Employee Experience (EX) Leadership

Build trust through employee experience and engagement

Nick Lynn

Contents

1. Introduction: The Leadership Trap

It's hard to lead any large organisation. Putting aside the business challenges that come with size and scale, it's simply difficult to stay in touch with what's happening on the ground.

As a senior leader, it's all too easy to become remote and detached. A close circle of assistants manage who you meet with. You spend most of your time with a cadre of other senior people who know it's in their interest to present things in an agreeable fashion.

It's difficult for your communications to have an impact. The things you say are filtered through layers of management. Like Chinese whispers, they have been thoroughly distorted by the time they reach the front line. This often reinforces your remoteness in the eyes of employees, who think you don't understand the day-to-day challenges they face.

Even if you make an effort to get out and about, your people know how to manage appearances to their advantage. You may sometimes smell the fresh paint in the lunch room when you make a site visit. That friendly employee group you met with was perhaps designed to achieve that effect.

In order to keep the organisation focused you reach out for help. The management consultants you hire are happy to give advice on how to restructure and transform your business units. Consultants are temporary partners with a focus on short-term outcomes linked to project goals. They will quickly move on to their next assignment. But long-term employees, with valuable customer insights and an understanding of work challenges, can feel overlooked and ignored. They may feel their experience is not valued as a result.

These organisational transformations come in regular waves and with soundbite names. This language is then incorporated into internal communications. This leads to employees feeling even more remote, as they're not up to speed on the latest jargon. Again, it appears as though senior management have locked themselves into an ivory tower of their own making.

None of these problems are new. They are inherent in any large organisation. Senior leaders have recognised these problems and tried to build solutions, so they don't end up falling victim to their own hubris.

In order to avoid this leadership trap, companies have invested in building trust through open and effective upward communications. Beyond other channels that may exist – such as hot lines, employee directors, unions and works councils – you need to keep an ear to the ground and ensure that you receive honest, unfiltered feedback. You need to be able to cut through the layers directly. You need to make sure that it's safe for people to speak up.

Over time, various devices have been put in place to make this happen. In the 1970s and 1980s, large companies began to routinely run employee surveys. These quantified employee satisfaction and allowed leaders to identify problem issues and hot spots.

In the 1990s and 2000s, surveys became fully-fledged engagement programmes, which provided all people managers with anonymous upward feedback. These survey activities were supplemented with things like focus groups, town halls, jams, open mic sessions, and so on.

This book looks at the rise and development of these approaches in detail. It takes the long view on employee surveys, climate surveys and employee engagement. It highlights some of the problems with these programmes and it pulls out the key success factors by looking at companies that do them well.

The best leaders have deployed these approaches effectively. They ask tough questions. They analyse the results in detail. They act on the feedback. They keep tabs on hot spots. They provide support to areas that need it.

I have been lucky to work with some great business people who are aware of how important it is to avoid the leadership trap in this way. This includes CEOs who read every single comment written in an employee survey. When I asked, for example, Ivan Menezes at Diageo, why he does this, he explained that there is no better way to keep grounded and to stay in tune with the day-to-day problems people face. Of course, being CEO of Diageo (the maker of Johnnie Walker whisky) means he can do this with a tumbler of something tasty to hand.

It's not easy to do this kind of thing well, especially when there are so many demands on leaders' time. But it is the argument of this book that it is more important now than ever to deploy effective listening methods and to avoid the leadership trap.

This is because modern organisations succeed or fail based on the work culture they create. Competitive advantage now stems mainly from the innovation, creativity and service that your employees provide. In order to free people up to do their best work, so they can deliver fantastic customer experiences, you have to establish high trust and open and direct communication.

The problem is that there are forces at play inside modern companies that make this difficult. Specifically, leaders have to manage a tension between pushing responsibility and risk onto individuals versus the need to build loyalty, collaboration, and strong teams and networks. Moreover, this tension is intensifying with trends such as automation, digital transformation, and the increasing use of contract and independent workers. Employees feel less secure, at the same time as leaders need them to contribute even more. The trust gap that results in many companies is a significant drag on performance.

This is why many leading organisations are exploring new and innovative ways of listening and creating dialogue with their workers. The good news is that internal social media, pulse surveys and people analytics mean that there are new sources of data that are available. These provide the means for more continuous listening.

This can allow leaders to receive useful feedback on an ongoing basis about the moments that really matter to people.

This is the opportunity provided by the new and emerging science of Employee Experience (EX). This shift, from traditional listening approaches, such as employee surveys, to EX data and analytics is the focus of this book. The aim is to help leaders understand how they can use EX to avoid the leadership trap, build trust and improve performance.

In all of this, the book is a mix of review, research and personal reflection. I have included old and new client stories, and I have speculated on future trends. It includes background and theory, as well as practical guides, best practices and tips.

The reason for writing this now is because I have been working in this field for twenty years. That feels like a personal milestone of sorts. So I want to look back over that time and pull out some key lessons.

It's also the case that the employee insights world is going through a major transformation at the present time (like most industries). So I wanted to take the opportunity to think about the future, both the opportunities that result from new technologies and data sources, and the potential risks.

Throughout my career, both as a researcher and a consultant, I have always believed in taking the long view on things. So I want to put changes that are taking place in the world of work, and which are currently much hyped, in the context of longer-term trends and developments.

It's clear to me that the new focus on employee experience builds on prior work on engagement, commitment and satisfaction that began many decades earlier and at a time when jobs, work and careers had a different set of meanings and expectations.

EX leadership refers to two aspects that this book delves into: those companies that are leading the way in developing this new science, and the key role that leaders play in shaping employee experience to build trust and engagement.

I hope that in this mix of stories and suggestions, there is something that you will find useful and relevant for your own organisation and your own personal reflection.

2. Individual Risk and Trust

There are good reasons for being optimistic about the future. In general terms, for example, Stephen Pinker argues in his book *Enlightenment Now* that life experiences are largely getting better. By many macro measures of human well-being, such as personal safety, longevity, economic security and happiness, people in many places are better off today.

When it comes to the future of work specifically, there are also grounds for being positive. Work places are generally safer. Boring drudge-work is increasingly done by technology now. This frees people up to do more interesting and creative tasks.

Many companies are paying more attention to their corporate and social responsibilities. There are stronger rights for working parents. There is more focus on gender inequality. There is more emphasis on inclusion and diversity.

In addition, people are able to work more flexibly. Not only in terms of where they work, but also when and how. There are pros and cons to this, but it can mean some people are better able to juggle their work and personal commitments.

Employment wise, there has been a growth in the number of small and micro-businesses. Small firms can now compete with big firms in niche markets by using social media and networks to sell their services. This is leading to a blossoming of boutiques and artisan businesses. These are often rewarding places to work.

In terms of positive thinking, some commentators even talk about a future democratisation of work, whereby technology empowers employees and enhances individual work choices. Some people hope we are shifting to a skills-based economy that is less restrictive in terms of how companies view their human resources.

To be open and up-front, this book is written by someone who is more pessimistic about the future.

There are advantages to pessimism, especially defensive pessimism, whereby you lower your expectations and prepare for the worst.

I might also spruce things up a bit and say that I have a critical perspective. Critical pessimism implies a firm degree of scepticism – the asking of hard questions about what's really happening in societies, communities and corporations.

In part this reflects my job. In my role, I interrogate data about companies to identify potential problems. This requires a critical eye. I have to be sceptical in order to understand what's going on.

At heart, though, I worry about the future of work. The basic premise of this book is that business is getting more challenging and that leaders need to adapt quickly.

Specifically, there are long-term trends that are accelerating and that have become critical to address in order for large organisations to continue to be effective. Not only in terms of generating revenue and profit, but also in making a positive contribution to the communities in which they are based.

From Built-to-Last to Built-to-Change

Most leaders I meet are also very interested in the future. There is a strong sense that many aspects are changing quickly and that most industries and businesses face disruption.

From a leadership perspective, many companies are planning for how they navigate volatile and uncertain times. This sense of uncertainty is not restricted to immediate political and economic events. It reflects a deeper loss of confidence in established business models and ways of working.

In 1994, Jim Collins and Jerry Porras wrote the best-selling business book *Built to Last*. The book was a celebration of the longevity and success achieved by some remarkable American companies such as GE, HP and IBM.

Despite its faults, it's one of my favourite books. The authors describe the success of these visionary companies through compelling stories. They argue that these companies succeeded by putting sustainability ahead of short-term profits. Their success is the result of leaders building the organisation first, rather than specific products. In their words, "clock-building" rather than just "telling the time".

These built-to-last companies are good at trying lots of stuff to see what works well. They set ambitious goals. They have strong work cultures. They emphasise home grown talent.

The authors talk about the myth of the great charismatic leader. They believe it's more important to have leaders who worry most about preserving the organisation's core purpose and values.

One of the attractions of *Built to Last*, and a key reason it became a best seller, is its focus on longevity when corporate survival rates are actually so dispiriting.

This becomes clear when you look at changes in the FTSE 100 index of the UK's leading quoted companies.

The FTSE 100 was launched in January 1984, just a couple of years before the Big Bang in the City of London when trading became computerised. Thirty years on, only 31 of the original hundred remained listed on the index. By the end of 2018, only 29 were still there.

Changes to the list over that time clearly illustrate the impact of globalisation. Through mergers, failures, promotions, demotions and new listings, the FTSE 100 has evolved to become a less UK-centric index. It now reflects the fortunes of the global economy instead.

In addition, the FTSE 100 has become less diverse in terms of industry. Whereas in 1984, there was a wide mix of manufacturing, chemicals and services, now financial services have a big presence.

Moreover, there has been a concentration of value, so that two-thirds of the value of the entire list is based on the ten biggest companies alone.

In the face of these trends, business writers have naturally begun to focus on other critical organisational success factors. In a twist of phrase, Ed Lawler and Christopher Worley in 2006 wrote their book *Built to Change*.

The authors highlighted how organisations need to focus on agility and transformation rather than longevity and sustainability.

In their words, "We believe that instead of pursuing strategies, structures, and cultures that are designed to create long-term competitive advantages, companies should seek a string of temporary competitive advantages through an approach to organisational design that assumes change is normal."

The focus on adaptability has increased in importance for all organisations. When leaders look into the future, they see even more upheaval ahead.

The new machine age

Of all the major forces impacting jobs and work, the most obvious is technology.

It is popular in business circles to talk of a fourth industrial revolution. Earlier revolutions refer to the rise of steam power and urbanisation, electricity and mass production, and computing and digitisation. We are now at the beginning of a new machine age and the implications are wide ranging.

This current economic shift is being driven by cognitive technologies such as artificial intelligence and robotics. It is fuelled by access to far greater computing power and massive amounts of data.

Erik Brynjolfsson and Andrew McAfee (who are both professors at MIT) describe three key features of the new technology landscape: platforms, crowd-based solutions and smart machines.

Firstly, in terms of platforms, companies like Uber and Airbnb provide examples of a new business model. These companies are able to create digital marketplaces where they act as a gatekeeper and charge a fee accordingly.

Secondly, new technologies have led to decentralisation and crowd-based collaboration. As digital technologies lower the cost of interacting, more things can be done by informal groups. In this way, for example, Facebook and YouTube can challenge traditional linear media businesses.

Thirdly, new machine technologies reduce the barriers to market entry, leading to start-ups and new competitors.

Market disruption of this kind is a haunting spectre for many executives. According on one study, 78 per cent of businesses believe digital start-ups pose a threat to their organisation, and 45 per cent fear their company may become obsolete in the next three to five years as a result. That's a lot of senior people who are even more pessimistic than I am.

As far as this book is concerned, what really distinguishes this new machine age is the impact that cognitive technologies will have on human relations and work.

Erik Brynjolfsson and Andrew McAfee describe how artificial intelligence is already being used to do many of the tasks that have until now been done by humans. This trend will accelerate in lots of ways, from self-driving cars to cashier-less shops to generative design. The nature of human-machine collaboration is changing and this has widespread implications for jobs and employment.

We are still at the early stages of this transformation. At this point, most companies (57 per cent) see the primary aim of automation as augmenting human skills and productivity rather than replacing humans at work.

In the short term, only 22 per cent of tasks inside most organisations are likely to be automated. But longer term, perhaps up to 47 per cent of jobs are at risk of automation, according to some studies.

The hope is that the jobs that are lost will be balanced out by the new jobs and professions that are created, although estimates of the number of new jobs vary widely. Moreover, there are significant implications for skills and training.

A key focus for many organisations at the present time is to break down jobs in order to identify those manual, high-volume, repetitive tasks which can be done by robotic process automation instead.

This can have a positive impact for employees. In call centres, for example, it can mean that routine requests are handled by chat and voice bots, leaving humans to deal with more complicated questions. These are often more challenging and interesting queries, requiring a focus on customer service and problem solving. In turn, this can help to improve the culture in call centres, which have often been difficult places to work in, characterised by low engagement and high turnover.

The work spaces that I have seen change the most because of robotics are factories and warehouses. In addition to the widespread adoption of lean methodologies, the biggest change in manufacturing is the introduction of smart machines and the requirement for computing skills inside the plant.

In a modern Coca-Cola bottling facility, for example, the level of automation is striking. A factory like the one in Baton Rouge, Louisiana is able to make and package 4.5 million servings a day, operating 24 hours, and once the syrup has been added the process is almost wholly automated. Robots even make up, wrap and then dispatch the final pallets.

Inside a BMW factory, humans no longer work independently from robots. Robots used to be fenced off and housed separately. Now robots are positioned alongside people. Robots complete the tasks that require strength or precision. Some BMW factories are also using exoskeletons to augment their humans' performance.

Amazon has become famous for its unlit warehouses where its Kiva robots move items continuously and bring goods to packers in a mesmerising fashion. When Alibaba introduced similar technology at its warehouse in Huiyang, China, it led to a threefold increase in output and a reduction in human labour of 70 per cent. You read that correctly, 70 per cent.

Robotic automation is already having a noticeable effect on the workplace, therefore.

Cognitive automation is still an emerging technology, but its long term impact may end up being far greater.

There is already evidence of a hollowing-out of middle income jobs in administration and service work due to cognitive technologies. There are fears that this is leading to job polarisation, whereby middle-income jobs are reduced in number, whilst high and low-income jobs remain less affected (for now at least).

Cognitive automation is likely to have a big effect on sectors such as professional services. The main area of growth in the legal sector, for example, is law-tech, which is receiving a lot of investment in cognitive technologies for things like contract and case reviews. This is having an impact on labour requirements, productivity and fees.

It is not just law. Similar changes are happening in financial services. Traditionally, investment management companies have been well paid for research and analysis, but in a world of open data and easy access to information, which can be analysed at scale by new technologies, that closed research model has come under serious threat (and has accelerated with regulatory changes).

At the same time, fin-tech provides new ways for customers to make investments. Fin-tech can provide personalised choices and recommendations. It offers a level of service and price that is sufficient for many customers.

Another sector that is being transformed in the new machine age is advertising. There is still a creative element to advertising, of course, but advertising has also become a big data game.

Global consulting firms like Accenture, whose roots are in accounting, are now among the biggest advertising agencies in the world. This is because the advantage in advertising now sits with the automated application of data science.

Traditional ways of understanding consumer motivation are being superseded by the real-time measurement of consumer behaviours. These can be quantified and analysed with probabilistic models that are developed and refined by artificial intelligence.

These capabilities are more often found in finance and accounting organisations than in the traditional advertising agency, which is why firms like Accenture are making great progress in the new realm of performance marketing (discussed later in this book).

In his book *The Globotics Upheaval,* the economist Richard Baldwin presents a concerning view of the future, where globalisation and cognitive technologies converge to have a dramatic effect on white-collar work.

Although new technologies have always destroyed some jobs and created new ones, in his view job replacement will struggle to keep up with job displacement this time.

According to Baldwin, this new revolution, driven by white-collar bots, is different for two reasons: "It is coming inhumanly fast, and it will seem unbelievably unfair."

It is already resulting in a shift in the balance of individual risk in many organisations.

Demographic changes at work

Globalisation and technology are disrupting many industries and organisations. Another important force having a major impact on the future of work and jobs is demography.

Demographic changes are already having a profound effect on the UK labour market. For starters, the UK, like many other developed economies, has an ageing workforce.

Around 32 million people are in work in the UK, but only 3.8 million are aged between 16 and 24 (12 per cent of the total workforce). This is the lowest proportion since accurate records started to be kept in the 1970s.

By contrast, around 30 per cent of UK employees today are older than 50. That is the highest proportion since accurate records began.

There are so many important issues wrapped up in an ageing workforce. What happens when people retire, taking their skills and experience with them? Companies need to identify, predict and manage for potential skills gaps and labour shortages.

Of course, many older employees may not be in a position to retire when they reach their sixties (or seventies). They may need to remain employed for economic reasons.

According to a survey by NORC (the National Opinion Research Centre at the University of Chicago) a quarter of Americans aged 50 or older expect never to retire at all, primarily for financial reasons.

According to another study, 42 per cent of Americans have saved less than $10,000 for retirement, while 14 per cent have absolutely no money put away.

Some older employees will also just want to work for longer, because they want to remain economically active for as long as possible. As a result, companies need to manage talent opportunities carefully, so that younger generations are not blocked in their early careers by older workers remaining in post.

Organisations need to adapt their working practices to accommodate the needs of an older workforce. This might include more part-time positions and flexible working. They may need to support older workers in maintaining their health and wellness.

All large organisations now have multi-generational workforces. For really the first time in the history of the modern corporation, four generations are working side-by-side in the workplace.

Age does not always infer seniority or experience. In flatter, less hierarchical organisations that have gone through significant digital transformation, workers of different ages can be working as team leaders, mentors, coaches and individual contributors based on their own mix of experiences and skills – not their age.

In terms of generations, millennial employees have been at the centre of a huge amount of discussion. In fact, to a ridiculous degree. Baby boomer leaders seem to have a strong sense that there is something different about these employees (basically their grandchildren).

Millennials have been stereotyped as lazy job-hoppers who expect everything to be delivered to them on a plate.

In fact, most research shows that millennials' approach to work, careers and learning is consistent with new entrants into the workplace generally and also reflective of broader societal shifts in attitudes.

The debate is also a bit pointless since millennials are already one of the biggest cohorts inside many organisations. In the UK as a whole, 9 million employees are millennials, which is 28 per cent of the workforce.

What is relevant is that the world of work is changing rapidly in front of millennials' eyes. They are at the forefront of the changes taking place and they are the generation that will be affected deeply in the new machine age.

As well as an ageing workforce and generational changes, the other important demographic shift is towards greater diversity in the workplace and (belatedly) many leaders' realisation that diversity and inclusion is important.

Diversity is broad in scope. Diverse workplaces are composed of employees with varying characteristics including, but not limited to, gender, ethnicity, religious and political beliefs, education, socioeconomic background, sexual orientation and geographic location. Diversity also includes cognitive diversity. In other words, people with different views and opinions, who are willing and able to express them. (There is much more on this in later chapters).

The leadership challenge

The forces described above – globalisation, new technologies, demographic shifts – are having a profound impact on work, jobs and organisations.

This shift is leading to an increased tension inside many companies.

On the one hand, there is a push towards greater efficiency and cost savings. Companies have moved work to low-cost locations. They are replacing human labour with technology. They are entering into new kinds work arrangements. They are shifting responsibility and risk onto the shoulders of individual employees.

But on the other hand, business success is increasingly dependent on making an investment in key talent and in creating a work culture where individuals and teams are freed up to innovate and to create distinctive value.

The key leadership challenge for tomorrow's workforce, therefore, is to manage this tension in a constructive way, so that leaders are able to build trust and create engaging experiences for employees and customers.

Trust matters

Trust is critical to the way every organisation functions, from the smallest start-up to the largest multinational. I believe all the projects I have run can be put under the heading of building trust, whether the aim has been to improve collaboration and efficiency, to encourage innovation, to increase customer focus, and so on.

Trust is at the heart of people's experience at work. A positive experience strengthens trust, but in order to have a positive experience there needs to be some degree of trust in the first place.

This operates in big and small ways. For example, a positive experience could be that my manager gives me useful feedback, which helps me improve the way I support a customer. I feel a stronger sense of achievement as a result. But I need to trust my manager to some degree already, in order to be open to receive the feedback constructively. This kind of situation is repeated throughout the work day in lots of ways.

Trust has always mattered to organisational effectiveness. But it's the argument of this book that it matters more for leading tomorrow's workforce.

This is because, in order to find a competitive advantage, companies are more reliant than ever on the ingenuity, creativity and ideas of their workforce. One effect of technology (the application of machine intelligence) is to level the competitive playing field in terms of products and services. In turn, this means it's literally the talent of your people, and the experiences they create, which sets the best companies apart.

As a result, you need to create an environment of high trust and open expression, so that people bring their best ideas forward. The organisation of the processes, systems and behaviours that are required to build that level of trust is really what matters.

What's meant by trust?

Before going any further, it's useful to have some definitions. Trust can be a hard concept to pin down.

In everyday use, trust means the reliability of someone or something. In academic circles, psychologists have viewed trust in terms of interpersonal relationships. Economists view trust in terms of contracts, philosophers in terms of ethics.

Much popular writing on trust focuses on the apparent decline in confidence in institutions like government, the media and business. There is a widely held view that there is a trust crisis in modern economies, which has profound implications for politics, for society and for the communities we live in.

This is compounded by the fact that traditionally trusted sources of information are being challenged by social media, which is vulnerable to misinformation, propaganda and lies.

There is also a broader, popular cynicism, characterised by the belief that the truth is always being spun to someone's advantage.

In fact, trust is hard to define because it always depends on the context and it changes based on the nature of a relationship.

One key concept is that trust is the result of a process, meaning there are phases and episodes through which trust is formed and eroded. As such, trust is cumulative, the sum of personal experience and recurring exchanges. There are key moments when trust is tested by critical incidents.

There are conditions that lead to trusted relationships being more likely to form at those key moments. For example, those doing the trusting need to have a propensity to trust and a degree of vulnerability, which is partly a result of personal characteristics, norms and incentives. Those being trusted need to have earned some degree of trustworthiness in the first place. This requires an assessment of their competence, integrity and benevolence.

Because an assessment is needed, trust is cognitive. In other words, it is based on what I know. Once I have relevant knowledge of your character, your competence, your reliability, then my knowledge partly constitutes my degree of trust or distrust. In this way, transparency and openness, as well as misinformation and bias, can influence trust.

Another key ingredient here is reciprocity, which means an exchange for mutual benefit. Or as Russel Hardin puts it, at the heart of a trusted relationship is the knowledge of encapsulated interests. By this he means: "I know you have an interest in fulfilling my trust in you (you encapsulate my interest in your own.)"

A general trust crisis?

The most obvious form of trust is between two individuals. Much work on the psychology of trust has involved measuring this, for example through game play. However, trust is also commonly seen as working across levels, including individual-to-organisation and even more broadly as generalised trust.

It is the perceived decline in individual-to-organisation trust that is felt to be at the heart of a trust crisis in economies like the US and the UK.

Much of the evidence for that decline comes from surveys, such as the General Social Survey run by NORC since 1972 and NatCen's British Social Attitudes Survey which has been run since 1983. Both surveys highlight a rising degree of scepticism towards institutions like government, business and the media.

In the General Social Survey, for example, only 17 per cent of people express "a great deal of confidence" in major US companies. This is down from 29 per cent when the question was first asked in 1973.

The score declined markedly in the late 1980s and then again in the early 2000s. Both periods were characterised by economic restructuring and shifts in the employment deal, including changes to labour relations under President Reagan and the jobless recovery under President George W. Bush. The score reached a low of just 13 per cent in 2010 at the height of the financial crash.

In the UK, the level of trust in government and politicians has never been very high. According to the Social Attitudes Survey, in 1986 only 38 per cent said that they trusted government "to place the needs of the nation above the interests of their own political party." By 2000, this had fallen to only 16 per cent. In 2016 the score remained low at just 18 per cent.

According to NatCen, "While a degree of scepticism towards politicians might be thought healthy, those who govern Britain today have an uphill struggle to persuade the public that their hearts are in the right place."

These words were written before the Brexit vote.

Another question in the Social Attitudes Survey is even more damming when it comes to generalised trust. When asked "How often do you think that people would try to take advantage of you if they got the chance?" a third of people responded "almost all the time" or "most of the time".

The communications firm Edelman has also tracked generalised trust through its annual Barometer Survey since 2001. Over that time the general population's trust in institutions like business, government and media has declined markedly and in 2017 Edelman concluded that, "With the fall of trust, the majority of respondents now lack full belief that the overall system is working for them."

In the UK in 2017, only 45 per cent of Edelman respondents indicated they trusted business. Only 37 per cent of people rated CEOs as "very credible" as a source of information.

At the same time, there was a growing gap between the views of those defined as "informed public" (college educated, higher paid, consumers of traditional news media) and the "mass population" (all others).

Many commentators have highlighted the importance of social media in this decline in generalised trust.

Social media now challenge newspapers and television as sources of influence and news. But incidents such as the use of Facebook data by Cambridge Analytica reveal the degree to which such sources are vulnerable to manipulation.

Online interactions clearly play an important role in the development of social capital, but more so in terms of bonding communities of interest together rather than bridging across diverse groups. Hence, the rise of social media echo chambers, whereby your own opinions are constantly played back by like-minded people, in turn reinforcing your own beliefs.

Algorithms also play a role here. The internet activist, Eli Pariser, highlights what he calls the "filter bubble" – meaning that as websites get to know your interests better, they also get better at serving up the content that reinforces your interests, while filtering out those things you generally don't like or agree with.

At the very least, the rise of social media means that traditional communication routes are breaking down. New approaches are required to communicate clearly and to cut through the noise, and to break out of your bubble.

This is especially important from a change leadership perspective and for overcoming the barriers to successful transformation, such as employees' overall scepticism and change weariness.

It has led writers like Sherry Turkle to argue that leaders need to re-focus on personal communication and direct face-to-face conversation. Organisations need to work harder to create both physical workspace and time for dialogue and conversation to happen.

Given all these challenges to trust then, how is trust affected specifically at work?

I argue below that there is a significant trust gap in most organisations, which acts as a drag on productivity and performance.

First though, it's important to note that there are two main ways in which trust manifests itself at work – in the functioning of teams and in the confidence that employees have in leaders.

Trust at work - teams

In terms of trust at work, one of the most important dimensions is at the local level.

Within a team, trust operates between colleagues and between employees and their direct manager.

There is a vast literature on high performing teams, which stretches back to the 1950s. But Jon Katzenbach and Douglas Smith wrote convincingly about *The Wisdom of Teams* in 1993. For them, effective teams are relatively small, contain people with complementary skills, share a sense of purpose, focus on achieving specific goals, have a clear approach to the way they work, and crucially, team members share a sense of mutual accountability. Two critical success factors are holding yourself accountable for team goals and following through on your promises.

It used to be that trusted relationships could be built up over time at the team level, based on recurrent events and reciprocity.

One of the most familiar models of team formation is Bruce Tuckman's model of group development, with four key stages: forming, storming, norming and performing.

The norming stage depends on a successful coming together and a settling down as team members get to know one another. This is when the team becomes focused and productive, with an established way of working together, leading to the performing stage.

However, in today's more flexible organisations, teams often come together rapidly and need to work together effectively without the time it usually takes to build trust in the norming stage. This has given rise to the notion of swift trust.

"Swift trust" refers to the way that rapidly-assembled or temporary teams are able to work together quickly. It's important because teams are often put together in order to achieve short-term tasks, before being disbanded and re-formed with different team members for a different task.

According to Debra Meyerson et al, swift trust requires parties to interact as if trust were present, and then to quickly verify that is actually the case in order to manage vulnerabilities and expectations.

As such, swift trust is a form of risk management. Swift trust assumes that members have little or no choice except to give each other the benefit of the doubt for the success of the group.

To build swift trust, the team leader needs to spend time setting things up correctly, for example, by explaining why each person has been selected for the project. In this way they act as a "trust broker".

It's important for team members to build a great first impression in the earliest days. Other success factors include dealing quickly with any issues as they arise, very frequent and open communications, and quickly celebrating achievements.

Swift trust is critical for virtual teams when there is limited or no time to build interpersonal relationships. It is especially applicable to discussions about the future of work, where projects may be managed by instantly-formed, diverse and short-lived teams of strangers spread across continents.

This may include a mix of different kinds of workers – employees, contractors, partners, customers – who only ever interact online. The ability to establish an identity, to share a common purpose and to deliver an agreed outcome requires an assumption that trust exists.

A key success factor is transparency and openness in the way people work. This is the hallmark of many virtual teams in the technology sector, for example, who openly share all their data and workings, as this means that trust verification can be quick.

At a team level, the key performance benefit from trust is improved cooperation.

In 2016, Bart de Jong et al published a meta-analysis examining the relationship between trust and team performance. Their paper looked at data from 112 studies, representing almost 8,000 teams and they found that intra-team trust is positively related to team performance.

A similar conclusion was reached by Sarah Brown et al who used the 2004 and 2011 Workplace Employment Relations Study to analyse the role of employee trust in influencing team performance in both pre- and post-recessionary periods. Their findings showed a positive relationship between three measures of workplace performance (financial performance, labour productivity and product or service quality) and employee trust at both points in time.

At a team level, therefore, trust helps people to focus on collective goals rather than their own narrow interests.

In high-trust teams, employees are more likely to openly share perspectives and to work through differences, improving collaboration and work quality. While in low-trust teams, people are more likely to spend time worrying about the need to defend their own personal positions and interests.

Moreover, in terms of the future of work, Christina Breuer et al have looked specifically at the impact of trust on the effectiveness of virtual teams. They looked across the findings from 52 studies, representing 12,615 individuals in 1,850 teams, and they confirmed the positive overall relationship between team trust and team effectiveness. But they also found that the relationship between team trust and team performance was even stronger in virtual teams. Hence, the ability to establish swift trust in virtual teams has an even more important impact on the performance of those groups.

Trust at work - leadership and confidence

The second key form of trust at work operates between the individual and the organisation they work for.

Francis Fukuyama argues that there is a significant economic benefit to trust for organisations. For Fukuyama, the most effective organisations operate like a network: "They can save on transaction costs substantially if their members follow an informal set of rules that require little or no overhead to negotiate, adjudicate and enforce." These informal rules depend on trust.

This is a link that others have explored in detail. For example, Paul Zak and Stephen Knack used data from the World Values Survey (WVS) to show how higher trust at a country level is related to increased investment and economic growth. Rafael La Porta et al also used WVS data to demonstrate the impact of trust on the performance of large firms. Marc Goergen et al used macro-level data and comparative evidence to show how country-level trust and firm-level trust have a positive impact on financial performance.

When it comes to individual-to-organisation trust in the workplace, there is a strong argument to say that the focus should be on confidence as well as trust.

Confidence is the belief, based on experience or evidence, that certain future events will occur as expected. Confidence means that I believe things will get better, assuming they need to improve, or that they will stay the same if they are already positive.

Confidence is future-oriented and it affects the personal and business decisions that I take. This might include, for example, whether I keep an eye open for job opportunities or if I will commit to stretching performance goals.

One key challenge for leaders in building confidence and demonstrating their trustworthiness is the increasing complicatedness of getting work done. It is harder to build a direct line of sight between input and output in modern organisations where individual contributions can be only a small element of a very complex work ecosystem. There is also a growing challenge of bureaucracy.

Yves Morieux is a writer and consultant who focuses on the increasing burden of complexity at work. He cites the causes of complexity as resulting from more stakeholders with more demands, more customers with more choices, more markets (domestically and internationally) requiring attention, more requirements and personalisation in service delivery, more difficulty in creating genuine value, and more conflicting demands and faster changes.

In turn, this causes companies to become more complicated in the way they work. They introduce more procedures, processes, structures, and so on. More time is spent on managing work and less time is spent on doing it.

As a result, many people feel they're working harder – in terms of being busy in meetings and on email and IM – but they're not really producing more.

In some organisations that are struggling with complicatedness, managers can spend up to 40 per cent of their time writing reports and up to 50 per cent of their time in meetings.

All this poses a productivity challenge. Fighting complexity, according to Morieux, is the number one battle for all business leaders.

Morieux is not alone in worrying about this. Gary Hamel is similarly appalled at the damage being done to the global economy by bureaucratisation. He argues there is a 3 trillion dollar wealth-creating opportunity in tackling bureaucracy, and pleads with business leaders to get to grips with it.

Some of the issues Hamel identifies include policies and processes sapping individual initiative, sign-offs slowing decision making, organisational boundaries creating silos, matrix structures blurring accountability, and time and energy consumed by unhelpful reporting and pointless meetings.

In my experience, complicatedness is the bane of modern organisations. Technology and globalisation have made it harder to do things simply and well. The chain of people, processes and systems that is required to deliver a product or a service can easily become long and convoluted unless you have real focus and discipline.

In some ways, this may appear counterintuitive. Surely technology is enabling organisations to be more agile and streamlined? Certainly, the Chief Financial Officer assumes this will be the case when making an investment in new systems. But in fact, human behaviour often dictates that things become increasingly messy, and too often organisations do not think through the human implications of technology changes.

In addition to the economic cost, the increasing complicatedness of work also makes it hard for employees to actually assess their leaders' competence. To what extent is the success of a leader due their efforts rather than just simple chance? It is often, frankly, hard to judge.

Individual risk

Another trust challenge, compounding the above, comes from changes to the traditional elements of jobs and employment, where more risk is falling on the employee side of the equation.

For the post-War generation in economies like the US and the UK, there was a fairly stable and well-established employment deal, which most companies stuck to. Sometimes the employment deal is called "the give and the get" or the psychological contract. Whatever you call it, it is a form of reciprocity.

In many organisations in the post-War period, in return for employees' hard work and commitment, employers provided pay and benefits, including pensions for life after work, as well as a career path based on experience, skill and seniority. In the US and other countries, health care for workers and care cover for retirees was also part of the mix. A represented workforce was an element in maintaining labour relations.

There were obviously problems associated with this deal, such as inflexibility and the tendency to reward tenure over merit. This compounded the issues that already existed in terms of a lack of diversity.

For these reasons and others, this deal has been breaking down over a long period of time. Certainly, the situation now is very different. For new employees joining organisations most aspects of that traditional deal are off the table.

Not many companies promise a long-term career any more. Instead, they offer the chance for workers to gain experiences and opportunities which will make them employable.

Benefits are more likely to be lifestyle-oriented, including things like gym membership, in order to ensure wellness at work. Other benefits are experiential, such as a college-like campus, or working spaces with creative meeting areas.

Rather than receiving a proportion of your salary upon retirement, an employee can expect a contribution to a savings plan (a defined contribution plan). When it comes to health care in the US, only a small number of large companies still offer retiree health care coverage.

Even the core tenets of a job are in question in some organisations, where tasks are being parcelled out among a workforce comprising not only employees, but also temporary contractors, agency workers and freelancers.

One effect of these changes is a lack of security and an increase in perceived individual risk.

According to the Work Employment Relations Study in the UK, 61 per cent of employees say they feel their job is secure. This number has declined over time. In 2004, 67 per cent felt their job was secure. This is interesting as the number of people in employment in total is quite high relative to long-term trends. Below this headline figure, it's possible to see more detailed concerns.

The UK Skills and Employment Survey, for example, explores "job status insecurity" – this refers to how people fear changes may affect their status at work in the future. Almost a third of respondents say they fear changes to their job will give them less say over how it is done. A quarter fear that changes will make it more difficult to use their skills and abilities. And 40 per cent fear changes will reduce their pay.

This lack of confidence has consequences. In the US, a study by Sarah Burgard and Sally Seelye looked at 25 years of data from the Americans' Changing Lives study to examine long-term histories of perceived job insecurity and its link to psychological distress. They found that insecurity is a significant predictor of stress and that this association holds after adjusting for age, gender, race, educational attainment and household income.

In his book *The End of Loyalty*, Rick Wartzman regrets the end of the post-War work contract. He argues that shareholders are benefitting while employees lose out.

Wartzman highlights the impact of off-shoring, outsourcing, new technology, and the willingness of leaders to lay people off, as among the trends that are leading to a new era of low loyalty and low trust. The impact of these changes is more risk for employees. "For workers, the American corporation used to act as a shock absorber. Now, it's a roller coaster."

In the UK, there is a lot attention paid to zero hours contracts, which seem to epitomise this new era of lower quality jobs. These contracts allow employers to hire staff with no guarantee of work. Employees work only when they are needed, often at short notice, and their pay depends on how many hours they work. The CIPD has estimated that 1.3 million UK workers are on zero hours contracts.

The headlines over the use of these contracts often neglect to mention their upside. For some people, especially those with critical and in-demand skills, these agreements can be very popular, allowing them to manage their work commitments flexibly.

However, for others, casual contracts like these are a concern. According to the CIPD, the most common jobs with zero-hours contracts are not highly-skilled technology jobs, but rather "administrative and support roles, care work, cleaning and various hospitality-related functions where people might not choose to be on them." In these cases, they can be a cause of stress.

Researchers from the Centre for Longitudinal Studies at University College London, for example, analysed data on more than 7,700 people living in England who were born in 1989-90 and are being followed by a study called Next Steps. They found that young adults who are employed on zero hours contracts (about 5 per cent of their sample) are less likely to be in good health and are at higher risk of poor mental health than workers with stable jobs.

Similar results were found by Brendan Burchell at the University of Cambridge, who looked at workers in two supermarket chains, one UK and one US. His findings showed that a range of flexible employment practices – not just zero hours contracts – contributed to anxiety and stress as a result of financial and social uncertainty. A key problem he identified is simply the insecurity of working hours, which is symptomatic of low-quality employment.

These kinds of issues attract a lot of attention, but they are only one part of the overall shift in the employment deal. The best organisations have realised that the psychological contract has been changing for a long time and they have worked hard to re-state their employee value proposition. What is clear is that, however you articulate it, all of the changes described here mean that more financial, career and personal risk now falls on the employee side of the deal.

The trends are not all negative for all employees, of course. Those employees with in-demand skills can drive a hard bargain. In areas such as data science, data management and coding, employees with these skills are able to achieve great benefits. These are the latest "hot jobs" and there will always be parts of the job market where skill gaps are critical, because supply is far short of demand.

In addition, although unions have less influence, there is a rise in new digital workplace activism, whereby internal concerns over workplace issues are brought out into the public domain through external social media. As more employees think of themselves as consumers, they are also able to bring a collective power to how brands and companies are perceived.

Witness, for example, how in 2018, claims of inappropriate behaviour were captured on WhatsApp from employees of the British fashion retailer Ted Baker. These eventually led to the CEO resigning after allegations of misconduct, including complaints of "forced hugging". Employees at Google have also demonstrated the power of online activism through walk outs related to the treatment of women and also of temps, vendors and contractors.

But for many people, the traditional equation that determined reciprocity at work, which was a characteristic of the post-War employment deal has been lost. Too few companies have come up with a compelling alternative.

What is the trust gap?

Having looked at the extensive challenges to trust that exist both in general and specifically within a work context, it is the argument of this book that in many organisations the result is a trust gap and that this is a critical problem for leaders to address.

Here, the trust gap refers to two key aspects: low trust and confidence in absolute terms, and a relative difference between the views of senior managers versus rank-and-file employees.

On the first point, in many organisations trust is simply low. This means not enough people feel trusted to get on and do their best and to work effectively in teams.

For example, in the UK on average, according to data collected by Willis Towers Watson, only 69 per cent of people feel their judgement is trusted. (Of this figure, 31 per cent agree their judgement is trusted and the remainder only tend to agree).

In addition, too few people are confident that company leaders are making the best decisions for the future. Only 66 per cent of people say they have confidence in the decisions made by leaders of their organisation.

This leaves a large group of people in most organisations – around a third of employees – who can be characterised as having low trust and confidence.

The figures are borne about by the CIPD, which has also been tracking trust at work though their Employee Outlook Surveys.

The CIPD found that only 29 per cent of employees rated the level of trust in senior managers as strong or very strong. Worryingly, more people (33 per cent) rated trust as weak or very weak.

On the second aspect of the trust gap, in most organisations there is a significant difference between how senior managers and rank-and-file employees view things.

Using Willis Towers Watson data again, 87 per cent of senior managers in the UK say they feel trusted, which is far above the overall average. Similarly, managers have more confidence in the decisions made by top leaders (80 per cent say they have confidence).

Edelman found a comparable difference in its Trust Barometer Survey, where 64 per cent of senior managers say they trust the company they worked for, but only 48 per cent of non-management employees agree.

This reflected a broader trend that they identified in the data, where there is a significant divergence of views between an "informed public group" (whom they define as those with at least a college education, who are very engaged in the media and have a high income) and everyone else ("the mass population").

Both aspects of the trust gap – low trust and a significant difference in the views of senior managers versus everyone else – pose a challenge for organisations.

There are implications for both team and organisational performance. There is also a significant opportunity cost, which is an even bigger drag in an experience-based economy.

Trust is becoming even more critical - a perfect storm

There is plenty of research, then, into the impact of low trust at work on performance, both at an organisational level and at a team level. So the trust gap that exists in many organisations, where around a third of people on average fall into a low-trust group, is a serious drag on performance.

It is the argument of this book that this should be a major concern for leaders. Moreover, given the changes that are happening in the economy and in the workplace, that degree of concern needs to be heightened, and quickly. Unfortunately, at the moment, many leaders see things differently from rank-and-file employees and are detached from the problem.

It feels as though there is an almost perfect storm affecting trust in organisations. The best leaders have long understood that trust-building is a core part of their role. But the challenges have intensified over recent times.

In part this is due to a decline in generalised trust and increased scepticism at large. This has been compounded by the fact that the complicatedness of work makes it hard for people to judge their leaders' effectiveness. At the same time the traditional employment deal has broken down and many companies have not articulated an alternative. Reciprocity has been damaged as it feels like more risk is now falling on the employee side of the equation. This is especially concerning for many people who, when they look forwards worry that automation will even further weaken their side of the deal.

On top of all of this, the problem for many companies is that trust has never mattered more to their success.

How do companies really win in the modern market place? In an economy where products and services can be quite similar, what really matters is the special element that your people bring through their own ingenuity, creativity, commitment and effort.

This shift is described in more detail later in this book as a shift to an experience economy, where goods and services are no longer enough to generate growth and success. What really matters now is the staging of compelling and memorable customer experiences. In turn, these depend on the experiences that organisations create for their own people.

The challenge for organisations is to remove the obstacles that are preventing employees from bringing their best thinking and their best efforts to their work.

Leaders need to enable people to go the extra mile in delighting clients, to bring that extra degree of empathy to product design, to insist on the highest standards when dealing with personal data or financial transactions, to think outside of the box when solving problems, and so on. All of this depends on trust.

Moreover, in the future, as more routine elements of jobs are automated, the human workforce will spend more time on the very tasks that require human intelligence and empathy.

Jobs are going to be more focused on creativity, critical thinking, and service, all of which are trust-dependent.

Companies will be competing against one another on the basis of the degree of trust they can establish with their workforce, and so the superior experience, service and design they can then deliver on to their customers.

What really impacts trust at work?

So what's to be done? The leadership challenge to building trust is pretty extensive.

It's the argument of this book that one of the most important resources available to leaders in building trust is employee voice.

Feeling you can speak up and that your views are acted upon is a critical ingredient in building trust at work.

Voice is a form of upward communication and is part of an overall culture of transparency. It is a complicated area, however, and in many situations employees will often default to silence unless leaders work hard to capture people's honest opinions and ideas.

It is an area that my work has been focused on for twenty years – enabling employee voice and encouraging leaders to listen.

The next chapter goes into depth on why it's important and what leaders need to do to encourage people to speak up. And essentially, speaking up is the focus of the remainder of this book.

In the next few chapters I look at how to run effective employee surveys and engagement programmes.

Later on, I highlight how the way leaders listen to employees and capture employee voice is changing.

Although many organisations have achieved a lot through initiatives like engagement surveys, there are now new ways of listening on a more continuous basis. These provide the chance to build trust and confidence. They yield immediate insights. They give a more holistic and dynamic view of employee experience.

I will talk about the opportunities in these new approaches and also – since I am a critical pessimist – the risks.

3. Safe to Speak Up

In the summer of 2004, The Coca-Cola Company was at a critical decision point. Trouble had been brewing for a number of years. Even to many outsiders it was clear that senior leaders were split on the company's strategy. Did they want to remain focused on Coca-Cola above all other things or should they become a company whose purpose was broader, to bring refreshment through a range of products?

There were heavyweight opinions on both sides. The company had become fragmented. Growth had slowed. Worse, their rival Pepsi had seemingly come up with their own winning strategy by branching out into snacks. There were also younger and more aggressive competitors in the market, like Red Bull, that had a more modern marketing style.

In the midst of this turmoil, I was delivering some pretty challenging employee survey results – the findings from Coca-Cola's first ever global Employee Insights survey.

Neville Isdell had only joined the company as CEO a few weeks before. As he reviewed the survey results he could see the scale of the challenge that lay ahead of him.

If the company's purpose was to bring refreshment and "fizziness" to people's lives, how could they do that when many employees, especially in the Atlanta head office, described the culture as like a government bureaucracy?

The results showed the "public pride" people had when they told friends they worked for The Coca-Cola Company. However, this was accompanied by a sense of "private pain" because it was so hard to get good things done.

So began one of the largest corporate transformations that I have been part of. Isdell engaged all leaders in building a Manifesto for Growth. He described the process as having the whole company "look in the mirror" in order to embrace some hard truths. He talked about needing to "reinvent the company". The Manifesto was an ambitious plan of building a portfolio of brands, whilst remaining focused on drinks and retaining Coca-Cola's distinctive system approach to production and marketing.

At the heart of the transformation was a focus on paying greater attention to employees – becoming a place where people felt inspired to bring their best ideas to work. Under the HR leadership of Cynthia McCague, they embarked on a huge culture change, which touched every aspect of working for the company. This included the physical environment, the digital tools people used, the way they recruited, rewarded and developed talent, and so on. It even included redefining what was meant by leadership, shifting away from hierarchical command-and-control towards encouraging performance and more open innovation. The Manifesto identified four key leadership capabilities to drive growth: brand marketing, franchise leadership, innovation and people development.

As Neville Isdell put it himself, "I dug into the employee engagement data and created some hypotheses and then tested them. The data said our people had no belief in management or in our ability to grow our core versus buying other businesses; some believed we needed to buy a management team that could run the business better. In August 2004, we had a kick-off with the top team in London to begin building what we began to call our "manifesto for growth." The senior leaders were confused at first about what I was doing. We had to confront our own lack of confidence – confidence that we could grow our core business, for example. It was a loosely affiliated team with distant relationships, but when they understood what we were trying to do they became very involved. They became a team. We asked them to dream a little. Then we asked, are we ready to do the work? After some real

35

catharsis we tapped into the passion and the caring. This initial work was basically repeated in a collaborative process over the next eight months involving the top 150 leaders around the world, engaging them in the creation of our future architecture and strategy."

It's a transformation that's still ongoing, of course, and the company faces new threats and pressures. The reason for starting the chapter with this example is to illustrate the power of employee voice and feedback. Coca-Cola began its transformation by collecting insights from across its entire global workforce. What that showed was the scale of confusion and misalignment, as well as some of the root causes. It provided Neville Isdell and Cynthia McCague with the ammunition they needed to light a fire under the broader leadership group and to create a sense of urgency for change.

It's a great example of how feedback can lead to a companywide transformation.

Empowering teams to accelerate change at Philips

Ten years later and I am working with another global organisation, Philips, which faces comparable challenges, but has taken a different approach to employee insights.

Philips was founded in 1891, originally as a light bulb maker, and had grown into one of the world's largest electronics companies. It was famous for a long list of innovations, including early radios and televisions, electric shavers, audio cassettes and compact discs. But by the late 2000s, its business had become sprawling and unfocused, vulnerable to more agile competitors and more challenging trading conditions.

After a difficult combination of events, including the tsunami in Fukushima, Japan, which affected its supply chain, Philips' problems were laid bare. In June 2011, the company issued a profit warning which shocked investors leading to a 10 per cent single-day decline in the share price.

Frans van Houten had re-joined Philips as Chief Executive in April of 2011 and he now quickly set out a plan to transform the company, which he called Accelerate.

As well as a focus on reducing costs, Accelerate was designed to transform Philips into a faster and more entrepreneurial company. According to van Houten, "Accelerate is all about delivering meaningful innovation to our customers in local markets – and doing so in a fast and efficient way."

As at Coca-Cola, with the shift in business strategy there was a focus on culture change and building a high performance organisation. In practice this meant breaking down silos, speeding up processes and working more simply from end-to-end. It also meant a stronger customer focus and doing a better job at differentiating performance.

However, one of the challenges for leaders was to break the strategy down into meaningful changes to the way people worked on a day-to-day basis. In my experience, there is often a gulf between corporate language (how the strategy is articulated to senior leaders and investors) and how most people really talk about things at work. This was certainly the case at Philips.

In order to help people translate the strategy into daily practice, van Houten and his transformation team set out three team behaviours they wanted everyone to focus on: be eager to win, take ownership and team up to excel. In order to engage all employees with the new behaviours, and to give people a chance to voice their opinions and to provide feedback, Philips ran a team-based survey.

The survey was short, asking employees a dozen questions specifically about the behaviours in their team. Results were only reported at the team level (although they were analysed on a corporate basis in order to measure progress). Each team came up with their own actions in order to align the way they worked with the behaviours. Progress on those actions was measured in the following quarter. The survey was repeated quarter-by-quarter for two years.

This was a very different approach to transformation than that taken by The Coca-Cola Company, which embarked on leader-led change. At Philips, the focus was on empowering teams. It was bottom-up. This meant collecting insights from team members and making it easy for people to speak up about what they observed and then to take direct action over the following months. The change was driven by lots of small pieces of constructive local feedback.

Philips' transformation has continued to evolve, of course, and has included spinning of its lighting business, which marked a historic shift for the company. Its focus on encouraging entrepreneurialism and high performance continues apace. But Philips provides a second great example of how employee voice can be encouraged in order to drive positive change.

When silence is dangerous: The Texas City tragedy

Both Coca-Cola and Philips illustrate the importance of collecting feedback and encouraging people to speak up. The focus at The Coca-Cola Company was on alignment and culture change. The focus at Philips was on end-to-end simplification and speed. Both companies encouraged employees to give their opinions in order to drive major change. Both companies established appropriate and effective ways for employees to express their voice.

The opposite of voice is silence.

Silence arises when companies do not establish good mechanisms for people to speak up or when the culture or climate is such that people do not feel able to express their opinions. What are the potential problems that can result? Unfortunately, there are lots of examples of where the absence of speaking up can lead to very serious problems. One area where this can often be seen is health and safety.

At 1.20 in the afternoon on the 23rd of March 2005, a series of explosions shocked the BP Texas City refinery. Fifteen workers were killed and 180 others injured. The explosions occurred when a distillation tower flooded with hydrocarbons and was over-pressurized, causing a violent release from the vent stack. Many of the victims were in or around work trailers located near the stack.

The Chemical Safety and Hazard Investigation Board report into the disaster identified a number of key safety issues, including trailers being placed in an unsafe location. BP paid a fine of 21 million dollars and they followed the recommendation of the Investigation Board to form an independent panel to conduct a review of the company's corporate safety culture. The panel was led by former Secretary of State James Baker III.

The Panel had a different remit from the Investigation Board. It wanted to understand BP's values, beliefs and underlying assumptions about process safety, corporate safety oversight, and safety management systems. The Panel sought to understand the "why" behind the observed deficiencies in process safety performance.

In order to assess the beliefs and attitudes of BP's workforce the panel developed and supervised the administration of a survey among BP's refinery employees and contractors. That survey was run in May 2006 (by my late colleague Gary Berger) and it included 7,500 U.S. employees and contractors.

The survey results showed that managers and white-collar workers had a more favourable view of the process safety culture than blue-collar operators and maintenance technicians. In Texas City, for example, 61 per cent of contractors and 56 per cent of maintenance technicians said that minor process-related incidents, accidents, and near misses were going unreported, while just 29 per cent of management thought that was the case.

A difference in views like this can sometimes be explained by a lack of feedback and by the common assumption made by many managers that "no news is good news". In fact, in any organisation there is a tendency for employees to default towards silence. Unfortunately, many managers are unaware of this and as a result do not do enough to overcome it by actively encouraging people to speak up and to give their opinions.

The Panel also highlighted the importance of employee empowerment, in other words establishing "a positive, trusting, and open environment with effective lines of communication between management and the workforce."

One of the recommendations of the Baker Panel was for refinery management to do more to "encourage workers to ask challenging questions without fear of reprisal" and to continue to "measure the effectiveness of this effort to improve process safety culture by conducting periodically an anonymous process safety culture survey." In other words, to work much harder to establish mechanisms for ensuring people are truly able to speak up.

The challenge of practical drift: The Space Shuttle Columbia disaster

In terms of safety culture, the problem of silence can relate to big-ticket items such as reporting incidents and concerns, but it can also relate to numerous small issues in the way that people work within their teams that can build up over time. A good description for this process is "practical drift".

Scott Snook's review of the "friendly fire" shooting down of two Black Hawk helicopters over Northern Iraq in 1994 has become a popular case study of the dangers of practical drift. There were a series of errors in the incident, as F-15 pilots misidentified the Black Hawks, an AWACS reconnaissance crew failed to intervene, the helicopters themselves were using out-of-date codes, and the Identification Friend or Foe (IFF) system failed. So a combination of factors came together, rather than a single root cause.

According to Snook, "What I found was largely normal people, behaving in normal ways, in a normal organisation. The story is one of a normal accident in a highly reliable organisation."

How can this be? Snook showed that among each of the parties there had been small changes to the way people worked and that local practice had drifted away from official procedure over time. This can be the case in any organisation. Small changes are made locally in order to improve efficiency or convenience.

Most of the time, these changes do not cause a problem and they gradually become accepted practice. But when they happen within the siloed confines of a specific team, they create systemic risks. At critical moments, those risks can be exposed. In the case of the Black Hawks this included, for example, using the wrong codes for months without ever being corrected.

According to Snook practical drift (or "the drift to danger" as it is sometimes called in safety research) is "the slow steady uncoupling of practice from written procedure." Behaviour that is acquired in practice and is seen to work becomes "legitimised through unremarkable repetition." It's a characteristic of any complex organisation and occurs when people adapt their behaviour to pressures over time.

Similar issues can be identified in most safety incidents. One of the clearest examples, is provided by NASA and the Space Shuttle Columbia disaster.

The official report into the Columbia disaster makes for sobering reading. On the 1st of February 2003, Columbia was destroyed in a catastrophe that claimed the lives of all seven of its crew. Columbia had taken off on the 16th of January, and when it was at 65,000 feet and travelling at Mach 2.5 a piece of insulating foam struck the leading edge of the shuttle's left wing.

The damage was detected during detailed reviews of launch camera videos and the crew were able to successfully complete their 16-day mission. However, on re-entry, the breach caused by the foam strike allowed superheated air to penetrate the wing's support structure, leading to the destruction of the shuttle and to the death of all seven astronauts.

The Columbia Accident Investigation Board was quickly established, in accordance with procedures established by NASA following the Challenger accident 17 years earlier (of which there were unsettling echoes).

As well as painstakingly reassembling 84,000 pieces of debris, investigators examined more than 30,000 documents, conducted more than 200 formal interviews, heard testimony from dozens of expert witnesses, and reviewed more than 3,000 inputs from the general public. The Board's conclusion was that "NASA's organisational culture had as much to do with this accident as foam did."

The Board described the managerial culture at NASA as having "an allegiance to bureaucracy and cost-efficiency." Again, there was a big gap between the views of managers and other employees. Although NASA managers confidently believed that everyone was encouraged to speak up about safety issues and that the agency was responsive to those concerns, the Board found evidence to the contrary.

41

Indeed, people had kept their concerns about the insulating foam quiet. "When they did not speak up, safety personnel could not fulfil their stated mission to provide checks and balances." As a result, "a pattern of acceptance prevailed throughout the organisation that tolerated foam problems without sufficient engineering justification for doing so."

For this to arise, lots of small pieces of insight were missing because concerns remained un-voiced. Problems were simply passed over. Worries were not raised.

The only effective way to combat the problem of practical drift is through active listening and by ensuring there are good ways to capture employees' opinions. Scott Snook refers to the importance of "leading by listening" and especially listening to dissent.

The Columbia Accident Investigation Board highlighted how meetings at NASA needed to change to ensure they provide an opportunity for people to raise concerns. "The leader of such meetings must encourage participation and guarantee that problems are assessed and resolved fully. All voices must be heard."

Hubris, denial and wilful blindness

The danger posed by silence extends beyond concerns with safety culture, as serious as those are. Leaders who do not succeed in encouraging people to speak up are at risk of developing blind spots and from falling victim to hubris and denial.

Hubris is a lovely word. The politician and author David Owen enjoys defining it as "exaggerated pride, overwhelming self-confidence and contempt for others." Lord Owen is interested in how leaders, especially political leaders, often suffer from "hubris syndrome". He describes this as "a disorder of the possession of power, particularly power which has been associated with overwhelming success, held for a period of years and with minimal constraint on the leader."

In my experience of working with hundreds of leaders and leadership teams, I would say there is a lot of hubris around and it's something we all need to worry about.

One very good thing about employee surveys is that they can be used to puncture hubris and to bring into focus some of the important things that are being missed or ignored by senior managers.

It's true that in any employee opinion survey, you will see a marked difference in the views of leaders compared to associates. Much of this is to be expected. If you're promoted into a leadership position within a company, you're more likely to be having a positive experience. In addition, you will have greater access to decision makers, you probably have more autonomy and you're likely to be better informed about what's happening.

You might also argue that leaders tend to be more positive by nature. In fact, that's a characteristic a company might even look for when making promotion decisions. So you would expect survey scores to be the most favourable at the top of the house and then to decline steadily as you review survey scores by job levels and, in fact, this is a common pattern.

In some companies, however, there is a cliff edge between the views of leaders and everyone else. In these cases, leaders appear to be living in a separate world, on another planet. When you see this pattern, it's often a warning of the existence of leadership hubris.

There are some key points in Owen's definition of hubris syndrome that provide important cautions. First, there is the assumption of power. In organisations where the management style is especially hierarchical, this can lead to feedback being withheld.

A key factor in whether people are prepared to speak up, if an opportunity presents itself, is the belief that it is in their best interests to do so. Politics and power are essential ingredients in that calculation. You can add into the mix that in many organisations seniority is correlated with tenure, so many leaders have been in powerful roles for a long period of time and are not used to having their opinions challenged.

A second key point in Owen's definition is that hubris can result from success. Success can blind organisations and leaders. It can mask a variety of ills. More specifically, success can create a halo effect. This is a form of confirmation bias where positive feelings in one area cause other characteristics to also be viewed positively and perhaps misleadingly.

This is something that Phil Rosenzweig points out very clearly in his book, *The Halo Effect*: "Much of our thinking about company performance is shaped by the halo effect. When a company is growing and profitable, we tend to infer that it has a brilliant strategy, a visionary CEO, motivated people, and a vibrant culture."

Of course, when performance falters, critics are quick to highlight the failings in strategy, leadership and culture that are suddenly obvious in hindsight. But until that reckoning comes, success often masks the true drivers of performance. This is as relevant for the people running an organisation as it is for outsiders looking in.

Moreover, not only can success blind people to the factors that led to it, but incentives may also discourage leaders from thinking critically about performance. Put simply, if results are good and you're being handsomely rewarded for that, then it takes a strong will to critically appraise the situation and to understand the role, for example, that good luck may be playing.

Of course, it's not just success that can cause leaders to fail to confront the facts. The opposite can also be true. Richard Tedlow in his book *Denial* highlights how countless companies manage to get stuck in a state of denial while their challenges escalate into full-blown crises.

Tedlow looked at numerous examples of organisations crippled by denial, from Ford to General Motors to Sears, and asked, "Why do sane, smart leaders often refuse to accept the facts that threaten their companies and careers? And how do we find the courage to resist denial when facing new trends, changing markets, and tough new competitors?"

The simple answer is that they ignore the obvious because they don't want to confront it. Denial is the unconscious calculation that if an unpleasant reality were true, it would be too terrible, so therefore it cannot be true.

Tedlow identified the leadership skills that are essential to spotting the early signs of denial and the actions required to overcome it. These include confronting the facts, encouraging straight talk, taking a long-term perspective and leaders needing to work much harder to listen effectively.

According to Tedlow, a key question for leaders to ask themselves is: "What happens to the bearer of any bad news? Do you shoot the messenger? Doing so doesn't change reality, but it does send a clear message that those who do voice disagreement or speak truth to power do so at their own risk. Which means you'll find it awfully hard to discover the truth thereafter."

Margaret Heffernan takes this view of denial a step further in her 2011 book *Wilful Blindness*. She argues that the biggest threats and dangers we face are the ones we don't see, not because they're secret or invisible, but because we're wilfully blind.

She blames the explosion of information and increased complexity of modern times, which pushes the human brain's capacity to assimilate information to the limit. This is compounded by human bias and our fear of change, as well as the focus on financial returns over people and well-being.

To counter these pressures, leaders require courage and perseverance. Leaders need to work extra hard to stay in touch with what's happening on the shop floor and they need to go out of their way to listen to complaints, for example through anonymous audits.

In fact, they need to institutionalise dissent by encouraging alternative points of view (Devil's Advocates). They should also ensure a diversity of perspectives and demand a range of solutions, for example by setting different teams to explore the same problem. Above all else, "leaders just being prepared to ask questions, can often stop organisational blindness."

Employee voice and silence

So far we have looked at how employee insights can be used to drive companywide transformation and how the absence of listening can result in problems. These can include practical drift, which creates a risk for health and safety. More generally there is the potential trap of leadership hubris and denial.

Across all these cases, the advice from people who have studied different situations is that leaders have to work hard to create effective channels for listening to employees and gaining useful feedback. It is not something that just happens. It needs to be a discipline and a constant priority.

In turn, this begs some important questions, such as why is it so hard to actively listen to employees and gain insights? What does it take to encourage people to speak up? And what are the factors that lead to people remaining silent rather than putting their ideas forward?

Over recent years, there is a growing literature on employee voice, which seeks to answer these questions. That there is a growing interest in voice is in itself important. It reflects the fact that as work and jobs are changing, the need to encourage people to speak up and to put their best ideas forward is more pressing than ever. Companies increasingly compete on service, innovation and effectiveness, all of which require constant vigilance and insight from everyone inside an organisation, as well as from customers and partners.

At the same time social media and digital communications are driving greater transparency and openness, which is altering expectations regarding employee involvement and suggestions.

Examining this shift in more detail is the final section of this chapter and the focus of the next ones.

Elizabeth Wolfe Morrison (who is Professor of Management and Organisations at NYU Stern) defines employee voice as: "Informal and discretionary communication by an employee of ideas, suggestions, concerns, information about problems, or opinions about work-related issues to persons who might be able to take appropriate action, with the intent to bring about improvement or change."

The content of the message can vary widely. On the one hand, it can mean identifying issues and concerns (problem-focused). On the other, it can include suggestions on how to do things better (suggestion focused). It is a pro-social or extra-role behaviour, in other words outside of the formal responsibilities of a job role. That's why there is a link to employee engagement, which is often defined as the willingness to go the extra mile in your job.

The target is upward in the organisation. For example, your manager or supervisor or another person higher up in the hierarchy.

Voice, in this respect, relates to mechanisms other than unions or works councils or employee representatives. And although related to whistle-blowing and upward performance feedback, the focus of employee voice in this book is more on day-to-day problem- and suggestion-focused insights from employees.

There are a range of mechanisms to amplify employee voice in most organisations and there are numerous examples included in this book. This includes things like road shows, skip-level meetings, jams, chat rooms, polls, and the like.

Even with new technology, an important informal mechanism for listening to employees is still some form of "Managing by Walking Around" (MBWA). MBWA was popularised by William Hewlett and David Packard and codified in their book *The HP Way*. Tom Peters also included lessons learned from HP in his best-selling book *In Search of Excellence*. Peters noticed that good managers tend to communicate more frequently, often informally with their team. He highlighted, for example, how Sam Walton, the founder of Walmart, believed in visiting as many of his stores as many times as possible, always making time for talking and listening to frontline staff.

The key element of MBWA is informal visits to an employee's work area in order to listen to suggestions and complaints, and then responding by taking effective action on them. For some managers, like Sam Walton, this kind of approach comes naturally. But for others it's a very different way of interacting and they may require support to be good at it.

Other mechanisms for capturing employee voice include employee surveys, engagement programmes and focus groups. There are many ways in which these are used. Employee surveys are often an annual leadership routine. Surveys and focus groups are usually integrated into change management processes, business improvement and quality management. Deming's cycle of Plan-Do-Study-Act, Total Quality Management, Six-Sigma and Lean production systems all rely on employee input and insights. Employee feedback is also a key part of 360-degree leadership assessments.

As a result, in large organisations there is often an infrastructure in place to amplify employee voice. But the effectiveness of all these approaches, of course, depends on trust and employees' comfort in speaking up.

Often, when trust, confidence, job satisfaction or engagement are low, employees are inhibited from speaking up and fall into silence.

Employee silence is the "withholding of potentially important input or instances when an employee fails to share what is on his or her mind." It is when an employee effectively sits on their hands. As Elizabeth Wolfe Morrison puts it: "Silence refers to not speaking up when one has a suggestion, concern, information about a problem, or a divergent point of view that could be useful to share."

The fact is that many employees often withhold their input and simply default to remaining silent. Numerous studies have shown that many employees withhold information because they feel there is nothing to gain or they calculate there could be something to lose by expressing their view. This is a problem for leaders, who can often assume that no news is good news. The fact is that you have to work hard to capture employee voice and to generate useful insights.

What affects the tendency to speak up or to remain silent? Given that speaking up is a discretionary behaviour, then commitment and engagement are important, as is an individual's sense of obligation, duty or responsibility. There is an internal calculation that people make regarding the pros and cons of speaking up, which also takes into account the probability of a positive outcome.

That calculation is affected by previous experience and also the shared experience of the workforce. This includes stories about events and experiences, which may have persisted for a long period of time. Being aware of and busting some of these myths is a critical task for a new leader or leadership team. I have worked in organisations where some myths have persisted long after those responsible for generating them have departed. In one company, the way that a leader had abruptly shot down an employee's suggestion in a public meeting was still being widely referred to ten years after the event.

Psychological safety

A key part of the calculation of whether to speak up or not is the perceived safety of doing so. It's not an easy thing to figure out how expressing your opinion might come back to bite you, since once an idea is expressed you lose control over who hears it. This is especially true in an age of rapid and viral social media. So the threshold for speaking up is potentially set quite high, as people err on the side of staying quiet. This is even more strongly the case, of course, for risk-averse or introverted individuals.

As well as individual level factors, on a group or team basis the act of speaking up depends on the degree of psychological safety that people feel within their work team.

Amy Edmundson defines psychological safety as "the shared belief within a team that it is safe to take risks." In teams with a high degree of psychological safety, team members feel able to express their opinion and to try things out and even to learn from their mistakes. Edmundson highlights the impact of psychological safety on important learning behaviours such as seeking feedback, discussing errors, seeking information and feedback from customers and others. These behaviours in turn have an impact on team performance.

Amy Edmundson began by studying medical teams at hospitals in order to find out what distinguished the best performing groups. She had expected to find that the top teams made the fewest errors. In fact she found the opposite was true. High performing teams appeared to be making more errors than low performing teams. She realised that this was not because the best teams were making more mistakes, but rather that people in the top teams were admitting to errors and discussing them more frequently. In other words, what distinguished the best performing teams was a climate of greater openness and transparency.

In 2015, Google published the results of a two year study into what makes an effective team. The project was led by their People Operations group and over two years they conducted more than 200 interviews with employees and looked at more than 250 attributes of 180 teams. The study found that effective teams were less defined by who was on the team (for example, the most senior people or those with the highest IQs) than by how team members interacted, structured their work, and viewed their contributions.

The five key dynamics that set successful teams apart from other teams were: psychological safety (taking risks without feeling insecure or embarrassed); dependability (counting on other team members to do high quality work on time); structure and clarity (clear, goals, roles and plans); the meaning of work (working on something that is personally important); and the impact of work (doing something that matters).

Of these five factors, psychological safety was by far the most important.

Google codified these factors into a team building tool which employees use to assess their overall team effectiveness on a regular basis. It's just one instance of the constructive use of voice at Google, about which more is written below.

There are other factors that feature in the calculation on whether to speak up or not. For example, these include the anticipated reaction of the target to speaking up. Will they be resistant or defensive? Will speaking up create discomfort for the target? And will your input be taken seriously? These factors get at supervisor effectiveness and capability, as well as the employee's relationship with other leaders in the hierarchy.

Some research has even highlighted how silence may stem less from an internal calculation than from automatic processes and implicit beliefs, in other words basic survival processes.

Jennifer Kish-Gephart et al have written about fear-based silences, which happen with different intensities. For example, anger and confrontation might lead a defensive silence or "freezing". In extreme cases, fear-based silence may become a habit: "Employees who have learned to tightly associate fear and negative outcomes with speaking up to authority may default to habituated silence without consciously experiencing fear and, in some cases, without even consciously registering situations as legitimate contexts for voice. When individuals have avoided considering speaking up for long enough, they no longer need the fear module to trigger feelings of apprehension or uncertainty to

50

choose silence. In such cases, silence that appears to be a form of resignation or acquiescence may actually be silence as a default – an unrecognised voice opportunity that non-consciously protects the self and avoids stirring up feelings of fear."

In listing the above factors, it should be clear that there are considerable pressures acting against people speaking up. As a result, the overall calculation of whether to speak up or to remain silent is finely balanced. The variables that can motivate or inhibit voice are extensive. Elizabeth Wolfe Morrison provides a great summary: Individual disposition (duty orientation may be a motivator while achievement orientation an inhibitor); Job attitudes and perceptions (engagement may be a motivator whilst detachment an inhibitor); Emotions and beliefs (psychological safety encourages voice while fear may lead to silence); Leader behaviours (openness versus a tendency to react angrily).

There are other contextual factors as well, such as accessible mechanisms which make it easy to speak up versus broader issues of culture such as hierarchy and power.

Taking into account the full list, the conclusion is that managers cannot assume an inclination to speak up. Rather, leaders need to realise that it requires deliberate, consistent and focused effort to be able to listen effectively to the opinions, ideas and suggestions that your employees have.

Voice as a cornerstone of the culture at Google

So what does that kind of effort look like? Subsequent chapters in this book highlight the most important means that organisations have for benefitting from employee voice and employee insights. A great example of the kind of focused action that is required is provided by Google.

Employee voice is one of three "cornerstones" of Google's corporate culture, along with meaning and transparency. According to Laszlo Bock who was Senior Vice President of People Operations at Google for ten years from 2006, "Voice means giving employees a real say in how the company is run."

There are numerous mechanisms for amplifying voice at Google.

"Googlegeist" is an annual survey of all employees. According to Bock, "It is our most powerful single mechanism for enabling our employees to shape the company."

Googlegeist asks around a hundred questions, focusing on innovation, execution and talent retention. About 40 per cent of the content changes each year to reflect current priorities and focus areas. On average around 90 per cent of employees take part and every manager with more than three respondents gets a report, which allows them to action plan with their team.

"There's a virtuous cycle here: We take action on what we learn, which encourages future participation, which then gives us an ever more precise idea of where to improve. We enable this cycle by defaulting to open. The reports of any vice president with a hundred or more respondents are automatically published to the entire company. At the same time, employee responses are anonymous (to eliminate sycophancy) and managers' results are not factored into performance ratings or pay decisions. We want employees to be scathingly honest, and managers to be open to improvement rather than defensive."

A good example of way in which this virtuous circle works is provided by Google's focus on simplification, which it called Bureaucracy Busters. In the Googlegeist survey employees said it becoming harder to get things done as the company rapidly grew in size and took on more corporate processes. The CFO, Patrick Pichette, ran a programme whereby the company asked employees to identify their biggest frustrations and to suggest ways to help fix them.

In the first round, 570 ideas were submitted and people voted more than 55,000 times. It turned out that many frustrations came from small, readily-addressable issues. For example, the calendar application didn't allow groups to be added, so large meetings took a long time to organise, and budget approval thresholds were set quite low, which required managers to review even very small transactions. As a result: "When we implemented the changes Googlers asked for, they were happier, and it actually became easier to do our work."

As well as their engagement survey, Google also runs an Upward Feedback Survey which asks team members to give anonymous feedback on their managers. Results are provided for a manager's development and don't directly influence their annual performance assessment – these are two separate processes. Most managers share their results with their teams. Managers can receive a Great Manager Award, the winners of which are asked to train other managers as a condition of the award.

The focus on manager quality at Google actually came out of an insights project that was led by their people analytics team, called Project Oxygen. The original intent of Project Oxygen was to try to prove that managers aren't that important. This was apparently a commonly-held view on a campus full of super-smart engineers who felt they didn't really need managing.

However, after reviewing employee survey results and thousands of performance reviews, the analytics team actually found that managers had a critical impact on things like employee attitudes, team members' performance and also employee turnover.

As a result, they identified 8 important manager capabilities, which act as a kind of manager check list and include things like establishing a clear vision; being interested in developing people; and focusing on achieving great results.

These surveys are one part of Google's focus on employee voice which is closely aligned to a second cornerstone of the culture, transparency. A key heuristic in decision-making at Google is a sense in which things should "default to open". This is a phrase that is often used in the open-source coding community and it means that things should, as far as possible, be public and available to all. You need a good reason not to share information, otherwise it should be available.

This is reflected, for example, in Google's performance management process, which it calls OKRs (Objectives and Key Results) and has had in place since 1999. OKRs must be ambitious, measurable, evaluated and, crucially, public. They are listed in your directory entry, which is visible to anyone in the company. The same rule applies to those in senior positions as to those in more entry-level roles.

This openness stands in marked contrast to traditional performance management processes in many companies, where targets are often unclear, key private and negotiable.

As Eric Schmidt, Google's CEO noted in 2014, "Every employee updates and posts his OKRs company-wide every quarter, making it easy for anyone to quickly find anyone else's priorities. When you meet someone at Google and want to learn more about what they do, you go and read their OKRs. This isn't just a job title and description of the role, it's their first-person account of the stuff they are working on and care about. It's the fastest way to figure out what motivates them."

With its emphasis on transparency and openness, therefore, Google goes to great lengths to enable employees to speak up. The company can still get caught out, of course, as it has over a wide range of issues, from diversity and inclusion to tax to privacy. In 2018, staff at Google walked out in a very public protest at how claims of sexual discrimination were dealt with at the company (among other complaints).

Interestingly, at that time, there was growing pressure to stop running Googlegeist, especially as the results were leaked to the press. But they continued to proceed with their focus on capturing and using employee voice.

No company is perfect. As Google grows in scale and becomes more corporate, retaining the distinctive campus culture that was established by the company's founders becomes harder. But Google provides a great example of the kind of sustained, collective effort that is required to take full advantage of employee voice.

4. Employee Surveys

As at Google, the most common mechanism for capturing employee voice in large companies is an employee survey. This chapter examines just how this came about. How did surveys become established as the main method of listening to employees and how has the content of surveys changed over time?

Not every company is as effective at running them as Google is, so it's also important to understand the problems that can sometimes come with employee surveys. Related to this, how have some companies managed to overcome any fatigue and keep their approach fresh?

The surveys says

I suppose it's not actually that surprising that some people are weary and sceptical about employee surveys or surveys in general. You get asked to fill them in all the time, but how often do you hear about how the results have been used? In an age of flowing data, they feel old-fashioned. A lot of the surveys you come across are badly written, full of loaded questions.

Public Relations (PR) firms can take some of the blame here. In order to generate awareness of a particular campaign, they love to run quick surveys that are turned into press releases. These are used to hook the media and provide easy stories. What's surprising is how many of these actually succeed. In any UK newspaper, you're likely to find articles based on PR surveys that are blatantly set up to produce catchy headlines.

Market research can share some of the blame as well. Many people find customer surveys annoying and mechanical. When I bought my car, the salesperson told me that I would be sent a survey by text and that I had to give an answer of 9 or 10 for it to count. They clearly understood how Net Promoter Scores (NPS) work and how to make the results benefit them.

Online shopping has led to a proliferation of requests for feedback from customers, which is leading to declining response rates. In customer surveys, response rates can be as low as 2 per cent. As a result, customer surveys have shrunk in length, often using just a few questions. Some market research companies now assume a maximum attention span of only 5 seconds.

Political polling is another reason. After any recent election, pollsters have been quickly hauled into TV studios to explain what went wrong with their predictions. This has become a regular post-election ritual.

In a recent poll about opinion polls – sorry, I couldn't resist – only 37 per cent of US voters said they had a great deal or a good amount of trust in opinion polling. In fact more people, 38 per cent, said they don't trust polls very much.

I am not going to review the methodology of these polls here. The point is that the number of surveys in the world has increased rapidly as the technology to run them has become easier and cheaper. There is a lot of noise as a result and a sense of fatigue. Because of the poor way in which many are run, there is also a lot of scepticism about their value.

Moreover, when it comes to employee surveys – the subject of this chapter – there are specific concerns that many people have. These often arise from having taken part in a poorly managed survey that didn't lead to any meaningful changes at work. There is also a heightened concern over respondent anonymity, even when a third-party agency is involved.

Lots of companies have been running employee surveys for decades. Large US companies began to use them in the 1970s. So they are not a fresh idea. They lack a wow factor at a time when people are looking for the latest new thing.

In many companies, an annual employee survey is a management routine. Just as with other management routines, like performance management, for example, they are hard to do well. They require senior leader sponsorship, effective communication, clear accountability, and so on. As a result, many companies do a poor job, especially when it comes to acting on the findings. This further damages credibility.

I am not going to defend surveys and polls in this chapter. But I do want to show that many companies have achieved a lot by running employee surveys effectively. I also want to put employee surveys in the context of an evolving industry of upward consulting. That industry is itself going through major disruption and in the rest of the book I will look at what's evolving in the new space of employee experience. I will argue that there is now a great opportunity to do new and better employee research and to produce more positive impact.

Employee insights

Most large organisations currently run employee surveys. A good estimate is that 90 per cent of the FTSE 100 companies conduct employee surveys routinely. The most common approach is to send a questionnaire to all employees once a year in order to gather feedback as widely as possible.

A large industry exists to support this effort. In 2014, the employee survey industry was said to be worth 1.5 billion dollars, employing thousands of analysts and technical staff in more than 50 different firms. Since that time, there has continued to be a significant investment in employee survey and listening technology. For example, in 2018 Microsoft bought the survey firm Glint, paying 400 million dollars.

One aim of this book is to look at how the field of employee insights is changing and how it will continue to evolve in the future. But it's also the argument of this book that it's important to put changes in context. In other words, to reflect on what's already happened and to learn from what's worked well. So it's important to understand what has brought us to this point, where employee surveys are routine and are used by most large corporations.

The rise of employee surveys

Employee surveys have their origins in sociology and industrial psychology in the US in the post-World War Two period. To some extent they are an American invention and they are associated with participative management.

Of course, the history of social surveys goes back much further. Their roots lie in the work of pioneers such as Frederic Le Play, the French mining engineer who studied family budgets and living conditions in early nineteenth century France, as well as the social surveys of William Booth and Joseph Rowntree in Victorian England. Thomas Bailey ran perhaps the first modern attitude survey for The Country life Movement in the US in 1908. This included sending questionnaires to half a million rural residents.

Robert Groves highlights two key eras in the early evolution of survey research. In the first era (1930–1960) the founders of the field invented the core components for design and data collection as well as the tools for analysing the results. As they were inventing the method, they also built many of the institutions that still conduct surveys in the private, academic and government sectors today.

One of the earliest pioneers was Daniel Starch, who carried out the first global advertising effectiveness surveys in the 1920s. Another was George H. Gallup, who founded the American Institute of Public Opinion in 1935, which later became The Gallup Organization. He famously invented the Gallup Poll method of measuring public opinion and he did much to bring polling science to the attention of the American public.

Another key figure was Rensis Likert, an American social psychologist. Likert is best known for developing the 5-point response scale, which is still the most common way of measuring people's attitudes in surveys today.

Likert worked at the US Department of Agriculture and then the Office for War Information before helping to found the Institute for

Social Research at the University of Michigan. He also founded his own survey research company, Rensis Likert Associates, consulting to corporations on how to improve management systems.

Outside of the US, survey research also took off in this period. In Germany, GfK was established in 1934. In the UK, the Market Research Society (MRS) was established in November 1946 in the offices of the London Press Exchange. Beginning with 23 founding members, early MRS meetings were basically lunches where practitioners of the new discipline would meet to share ideas and the latest developments.

A golden era for employee research

The second era (1960–1990) witnessed a vast growth in the use of surveys. This really was a golden era for survey research in general.

Growth was in part due to interest in monitoring the impact of social change. There was a blossoming of mathematical approaches in social science more generally, which is sometimes referred to as the Quantitative Revolution. There was also a growing demand from businesses to use data to study consumer and employee behaviours.

During this period, The National Opinion Research Center (NORC) at the University of Chicago began to run its General Social Survey (GSS) in 1972. The GSS monitors social change and the complexity of American society. The survey plays an important role in American sociology. In fact, after the US Census, it is the second most frequently analysed source of information for the social sciences in the United States.

The British Social Attitudes Survey (SAS) was also established in this period, in 1983 by the National Centre for Social Research (NatCen). The SAS involves in-depth surveys focused on key policy areas such as education, the labour market, crime and media.

There was also a proliferation of market research companies during this era. In the UK, for example, Taylor Nelson was established in 1965 and MORI (Market & Opinion Research International) was founded in 1969. MORI went on to become the largest independent research organisation in the country.

Ipsos (who ended up buying MORI in 2005) was founded in France in 1975. Also in France, Sofres (which merged with Taylor Nelson in 1997 before both became part of WPP) was established in 1964. Through various waves of consolidation, which are still ongoing, these companies remain some of the largest market research agencies today.

In the employee survey field specifically, this period saw the foundation of the firms that would shape the industry. Sirota was founded by David Sirota in New York in 1972. It was the first of a group of firms focused on running employee surveys that emerged in the USA in the 1970s and 1980s.

International Survey Research (ISR) was founded in 1974 in Chicago by Jack and Gay Stanek. Valtera was established by Bill Macey (also in Chicago) in 1977. Gantz-Wiley was founded by Jack Wiley and Gail Gantz in Minneapolis in 1986.

These employee survey firms had their origins in industrial psychology and sociology. They hired PhDs as Project Directors and applied scientific principles to the study of morale, employee satisfaction, commitment and (latterly) engagement. Informed by management thinkers like Peter Drucker and Edward Deming, they tackled issues to do with deteriorating industrial relations, work quality, organisational change and globalisation.

The growth in surveys was enabled by new technologies. Computers were used to process survey results in the early 1960s. Computer-assisted telephone interviewing began in the late 1960s. Interactive voice response (telephone) technology and optical mark recognition scanning started to be used in the 1980s.

The pioneer employee survey companies made a great contribution by introducing a discipline of listening to employees in many large organisations. They formed an industry based on providing upward consulting solutions. In other words, they captured insights from staff on the shop floor and played them back to leaders in the corporate head office who were often far removed from what was happening both in terms of physical distance and management levels. The primary tool was opinion surveys using Likert-style response scales. The surveys were often long and comprehensive, sometimes over 100 questions in length.

There was a lot of variety in survey content. Although there was a focus on measuring morale and employee satisfaction, other questions were tailored to a company's specific business priorities. Typically, in an employee survey process, there would be a round of stakeholder interviews in order to create bespoke questions that were aligned to a particular company's hot topics. It was worth making that investment in survey design, since allowing employees time during the work day to complete a 30-minute questionnaire is a significant business cost.

Crucially, this meant that surveys were designed to answer specific questions that leaders had. These questions were business-focused rather than HR-driven. Examples include, encouraging more innovation, embedding a stronger customer focus, breaking down organisational silos, building alignment across diverse business units, and so on.

Surveys at this point were often referred to as climate surveys. Over time, climate has become a less-frequently used term than culture in an organisational setting, but climate surveys were designed to explore people's descriptions of how the organisation functions. They capture employees' immediate perceptions of day-to-day interactions and events.

In the early days, questionnaires were administered on paper, which required the survey companies to build a supply chain to oversee printing, distribution and data entry.

The employee survey companies built relational databases and developed their own benchmarks. This was a more profitable route than trying to develop standards or to coordinate consortium-style approaches.

Benchmarks helped to take account of some key biases in survey results, such as how responses vary by country or function or job role. Most survey companies also developed some kind of high-performance benchmark to help leaders set ambitious targets. In turn, these goals would be used as key performance indicators in a balanced business scorecard, which was a popular management tool at the time.

During this period, the employee survey industry was in a phase of expansion. Many clients were running employee surveys for the first time. So the process of introducing the survey internally was important and involved extensive education, and training. There was a high degree of dependence on the expertise of the employee survey firms as there was little internal experience to draw upon on the client side.

In multinational companies during this period, there was often a piecemeal approach to surveying. Countries and business units ran different surveys at different times, often using different providers. This reflected the needs and focus areas of different markets, but it made global analysis and reporting difficult to do.

The growth of the group of pioneer employee surveys firms was driven by geographical expansion, rather than innovation in their approach. The founders travelled around the world with briefcases full of example surveys and a well-honed pitch. As a result, they established small offices in different world cities in order to provide services in local languages and in respect of local work cultures.

The employee engagement era

In the 1990s, employee research began to evolve again. Probably the key moment was the phenomenal success of the book *First, Break All the Rules*. Written by Marcus Buckingham and Curt Coffman from Gallup, it became a best seller and one of the most influential management books of the time. It was based on findings from interviews and lots of Gallup employee survey results. It used regression and factor analysis to identify key behaviours associated with good people management.

The research for the book also led to a short 12-question employee survey, which Gallup marketed aggressively and as part of an overall management development programme. For the first time on a large scale, employee surveys were simplified, standardised and packaged for a global buyer.

First, Break All the Rules also popularised the term employee engagement, which became a business buzzword.

It's worth reflecting a little on the evolution of research topics, which shifted over time from morale to job satisfaction, to commitment and then to engagement.

Morale and motivation theory

The previous era's focus on morale and commitment actually dated back to interest in troop morale, as well as the impact of propaganda on the general population during World War II. This work had infused US sociology departments and it greatly influenced the founders of the original employee survey firms.

However, morale was a broad and general term, which included concepts like team spirit and cohesion. Over time, the specific elements of morale began to be unpacked and looked at separately, within a corporate and business environment. These dimensions included organisational climate, employee involvement and job satisfaction.

The interest in job satisfaction was also the result of work in psychology and new theories of employee motivation. The organisational psychologist Frederick Herzberg had a huge influence on employee research in this period. His writing also affected a broader audience that had a growing interest in corporate leadership effectiveness. Herzberg's 1968 publication "One More Time, How Do You Motivate Employees?" is one the most-requested Harvard Business Review articles of all time.

Herzberg's motivator-hygiene theory looked in depth at satisfaction and motivation in the workplace. His theory stipulated that satisfaction and dissatisfaction are driven by different factors.

Motivating factors are those that make people want to perform at their best, such as accomplishing challenging tasks, being recognised for doing a great job and gaining advancement as a result.

Hygiene factors are those that, if you do not get them right, can lead to dissatisfaction and a sense of unfairness. They include things like pay, benefits and physical working conditions.

Following this train of thought, employee surveys often focused on understanding both sets of factors and identifying opportunities and risks.

Related to this, another important element of early employee survey work was an interest in improving labour relations. Large corporations wanted to establish a direct channel for employees' opinions, so they did not have to rely on union representatives. In addition, by understanding potential problems with hygiene factors, which could lead to dissatisfaction and feelings of unfairness, leaders hoped that their personnel departments could find ways to avoid strikes and stop any further unionisation. This was especially true during the time of huge turmoil in industrial relations in the US and the UK in the 1970s and 1980s.

Commitment and engagement

At the end of the 1980s, the focus of employee surveys evolved to look more at commitment. Rather than addressing hygiene factors, employee commitment was concerned with the degree of attachment that employees had towards the organisation they worked for. It was focused on alignment, affiliation and notions of corporate citizenship, which were all seen as key elements of overall organisational effectiveness (itself a burgeoning field).

In 1990, William Kahn used the term employee engagement in his paper "Psychological Conditions of Personal Engagement and Disengagement at Work." He was among the first to do so as he focused on the connection between employees' selves and their work roles.

Interestingly, he later explained why he had used the term: "I used engagement and disengagement because those words evoke very clearly the movements that people make toward and away from their work, other people and the roles that they had. Engagement is a word that suggests betrothal – the decision to commit to a role, an identity and a relationship that offers fulfilment."

In 1991, Natalie Meyer and John Allen published research into a three-component model of organisational commitment that also had a great influence on employee research. The first of their three factors was an affective component. This referred to employees' emotional attachment to, identification with, and involvement in their organisation.

Their second factor was a continuance component, which referred to the extent to which an employee perceives that leaving the organisation would be too costly. Employees with strong continuance commitment remain because they feel that they have to do so.

The third component was normative, which referred to an employee's feelings of obligation to their company and the belief that staying is the right thing to do. Employees with strong normative commitment remain because they feel it's what they ought to do.

As a result of all this writing, many employee surveys began to focus intensively on issues like pride, advocacy and individual alignment to their organisation's goals and values.

In addition, many employee survey firms began to describe their approach in terms of three parts. For example, the consulting firm Hewitt came up with their model of Say, Stay, Strive, and ISR and Sirota measured how employees Think, Feel and Act.

In addition to affiliation, there was an increased focus on retention and loyalty. Surveys began to ask employees about their intention to stay or leave their employer. In part, this reflected a rising sense that key talent really mattered to organisational performance. McKinsey, for example, started talking about a "war for talent" in 1997.

In 1998, Harvard Business Review published research which cemented the value of engagement and commitment. This was research by the US department store Sears into what was called the service-profit-chain. As part of their overall business transformation at the time, Sears used statistical modelling to review a series of performance indicators from across 800 stores. Their analysis showed how department stores that had high levels of individual employee commitment (they referred to "attitude about the job" and "attitude about the company") also tended to have better customer impressions and sales performance. They quantified that a 5 unit increase in employee attitudes could drive a 1.3 unit increase in customer impression, which could deliver a 0.5 per cent increase in revenue growth. This kind of maths began to get serious leadership attention.

Engagement surveys

On the back of all this, Gallup marketed its 12-item questionnaire as an employee engagement programme, and they were really the first company to do so.

In *First, Break All the Rules,* the authors don't really discuss what they mean by engagement specifically, but they did identify different levels of engagement inside most companies: "An engaged employee is one that's passionate about their work, feels connected to the business and is driving forward with innovation, progress and goals."

By contrast, when an employee is not engaged, "they're in a "checked out" mode. They show up for work each day and do their tasks, but aren't passionate, innovative or making deeper contributions."

Even worse, are those who are actively disengaged: "Not only are these employees deeply unhappy, but they're acting out and may be working against the organisation's objectives on a daily basis."

The success of the marketing of employee engagement, which is discussed in more detail in the next chapter, meant that packaged engagement surveys really took off in the 2000s.

Engagement surveys were now being sold by a wide range of different companies from communications and PR agencies through to technology firms and even strategy consultants like McKinsey who produced their own packaged survey, the Organisational Health Index, in 2010.

This period also saw a proliferation of lists of the best places to work, great places and admired companies, and a whole series of employee engagement awards and events.

The term engagement also moved out of the HR world and into the vocabulary of Internal Communications.

Internal communications was, for a long time, a very traditional function inside many large companies. The poor relation to Corporate Affairs (external communications), internal communications was tasked with formally disseminating company news to staff through bulletins and newsletters.

As electronic communication channels proliferated and as communications became linked with restructuring and change management, the function embraced more of an advertising and marketing mindset. This included brand-centred campaigning and stakeholder management.

In many instances now, employee engagement simply means "good internal communications". A Director of Employee Engagement is as likely to sit in the communications function as they are in HR (although, in many companies the two functions are sensibly fused together).

Employee engagement is also incorporated into notions of good corporate governance and into professional standards in HR by organisations like the CIPD and Investors in People in the UK. Employee engagement measurement has become a required discipline in some regulated industries. It is an important element of quality management programmes like the European Foundation for Quality Management.

Alongside the shift in focus onto employee engagement, the internet provided the great technological disruption in this era. Employee survey firms moved into online surveys and electronic results reports.

As more companies used HR Information Systems (HRIS), it became possible to pre-code online surveys, which improved accuracy. Previously, most employee surveys had required respondents to self-identify their department, location, length of service, and so on. Sometimes people made mistakes or they might deliberately misidentify themselves, if they did not trust the process.

The use of HRIS meant that this coding could be captured automatically. It also meant that additional talent information could be analysed, such as performance rating or high potential status. In this way, you can understand the flight risk of some of your most important employees.

Whereas climate surveys may have included 100 questions, engagement surveys tended to be shorter, typically around 30-40 questions. The content was often focused on factors relating to your team and your boss. A shorter survey was quicker to complete and less costly in terms of the time required to take people off the line.

It also meant there was less data for managers to analyse when they received the results, which, in turn, simplified local action planning.

It's worth noting that engagement surveys remained far longer than questionnaires used in customer research. This reflects the fact that completing a company-run engagement survey is seen as a duty, part of your responsibilities as an employee. As a result, response rates are also much higher in employee than customer research, typically over 80 per cent.

Engagement surveys are anonymous in order to ensure honest feedback. The primary way employees' responses are kept anonymous is through only producing aggregate scores for groups. In the earlier era of employee research, most companies followed a standard group reporting size of 10 people. In the engagement era, the group size was often reduced, sometimes down to seven or even five respondents. This reflected an appetite for more local data, in part because managers were including engagement objectives in their performance plans. It also reflected a shift to smaller teams in some organisations.

Online technology also opened up opportunities for new and different kinds of research and there was a blurring of the lines as the original employee survey firms aligned themselves with consulting partners, moved into measuring customer engagement, began to run assessments for recruitment, and collected 360-degree feedback for leadership development.

By the 2000s, the pioneer employee survey firms had ageing owners, they faced new competitors and they required significant investment in technology in order to deliver a better online user experience.

Gantz-Wiley was acquired by one of those new competitors (Kenexa) in 2006. Kenexa itself became part of IBM in 2012. Valtera was acquired by CEB in 2006. ISR was acquired by Towers Perrin in 2007. The original pioneer firm, Sirota, became part of Mercer in 2016. This wave of buy-outs and consolidation ushered in a new era of disruption and change for the employee survey industry.

5. Employee Engagement

Employee engagement programmes have emerged as a common way of using employee insights in most large companies. They provide a key mechanism for building trust and for improving team and organisational effectiveness. They're one way of making it safe for people to speak up.

This chapter shows how companies can achieve a lot by focusing on employee engagement. It includes case studies from companies that have used surveys to drive significant positive change, even across workforces that are traditionally hard to reach, such as factories, the railways and call centres.

It then goes on to review the key success factors in using engagement surveys to affect transformation and change in any company. That's what really matters in all engagement programmes – the survey itself is far less important than the impact the whole exercise has on employee trust and business performance.

Building Nomad Foods

The first example is from the food industry. There are specific business and engagement challenges in the sector, where companies are focused on issues such as agility, quality and innovation.

For one thing, these companies have a lot of employees in manufacturing roles where line management can be a challenge.

In combination with operating effectiveness, these companies also have to have a focus on marketing and brand building. With few direct channels to consumers, they mainly work through retailers for marketing control of shelf space as well as the "mindspace" of distributors and consumers.

Consumer preferences are changing. Consumers want foods that are not only good for them, but that are also good for the environment and for local communities. So corporate social responsibility is an important priority, alongside other core concerns such as affordability, food safety and traceability.

Most companies have a focus on innovation and differentiation, but bringing new products to market takes time. In an industry where large companies dominate, smaller companies can be faster and better able to build new brands that stand out.

Employees tend to have lots of pride in their local brands, but their affiliation to their parent or holding company is usually far weaker. Given the waves of restructuring that have taken place as the industry consolidates, job security tends to be low.

One company that has worked on engagement very effectively in order to overcome some of these industry challenges is Nomad Foods.

Nomad Foods has grown into the biggest frozen food company in Europe. The company was formed in 2015, by private equity, and embarked on a series of mergers and acquisitions. It has a rich heritage and iconic brands such as Birds Eye, iglo and Findus. It employs 4,800 people in 13 countries, with a dozen factories. Its success is built on a reputation for innovation and understanding what the consumer wants from frozen food.

A key pillar of the company's long-term financial strategy is to deliver sustainable organic top and bottom line growth by combining global scale and local proximity to consumers and customers. They also have a focus on brand heritage, innovation and developing strong retail partnerships. With 38 per cent of net revenue coming from sea food there is a natural focus on nutrition and sustainable sourcing.

From a people perspective, the aim is to build a high performance culture. This means encouraging and rewarding entrepreneurial and team behaviour, and creating an inspiring work place where individuals and teams can be successful.

There has been a major focus on organisation building, in other words creating one, strong company out of its component parts. Alongside this, there has been a shift in leadership thinking, from acting like a private equity venture (where you buy in talent and fast-growing brands) to identifying talent and growth opportunities from within the organisation itself.

A year after Nomad Foods' formation, the company rolled out its new "Our Way" values in order to accelerate this change in mindset. At almost three times the size of their nearest competitor, the values are designed to make sure the organisation stays focused on being "fast, nimble and entrepreneurial." The values include things like "act fast" and "always striving".

According to Tim Kensey, HR Director Corporate & Engagement, "The Our Way values are a key statement of what's important to us as a business and also the behaviours that are required to drive our future success. After launching the values to the new organisation, we wanted to run a survey to establish a base line and to understand how and where we should focus to improve."

The "Our Way, Our Voice" survey was one of the first global initiatives for the new organisation. As a result of the survey, the executive team identified three focus areas: leadership, learning and development, and communication.

In terms of leadership, they focused on increasing the visibility of the executive committee through site visits and town halls. Executive team meetings were held outside of their headquarters and in different locations throughout the year.

They also introduced, for the first time, companywide leadership standards. These established a common set of behaviours against which leaders' performance could be judged. They were a way of making the values more practical for leaders, managers and employees.

When they were first launched, the values were effectively a statement of intent. The survey results indicated the need for a second phase, where the values were brought to life more clearly by defining practical, day-to-day ways of working.

71

This also led to an evolution of their existing recognition scheme, called People Awards. Throughout the year, employees who really demonstrate they live the values are identified locally. The best examples are then recognised on a companywide basis. This includes an annual ceremony to celebrate those individuals. They also recognise their best people managers. Importantly, this is done at the same event that celebrates other key business successes, such as Factory of the Year. It is not a separate HR exercise.

The second focus area was learning and development. The company introduced new line manager and leadership academies. Around 200 people went through the programme in its first eighteen months. This was their first major investment in internal talent and represented a clear shift from the world of a private equity organisation, where it is more common to buy-in talent.

According to Tim, "This was partly about bringing our promises to life." Moreover, "All these efforts are about creating more of a "glue" across all of the organisation. They're designed to make people think companywide from the outset. We want to establish a One Company feeling."

A key part of this effort is improved communications. One of their biggest challenges has been the absence of a common digital platform. This made it harder to integrate some of their acquisitions, which remained on legacy systems. The company invested in a new common communication platform called "Nomad and Me". This is accessible to all employees, even those working in factories. They have also invested in messaging and collaboration tools.

Another approach that has been very successful is ambassador networks. To begin with, they established Our Way Value Ambassadors. These were employees from different sites and functions (so not HR people) who performed a critical role in embedding the values. They tested different approaches and fed back their learnings, they shared best practices and success stories, and they benchmarked various programmes. They had a focus on bringing the values to life. They acted as role models.

Effectively, they were more "glue" for the organisation. The approach has been so successful that the company now also has ambassadors for inclusion and diversity, sustainability, and health and wellness.

The company believes that what gets measured gets done, so they set targets based on making quick progress in their focus areas as well as on employee engagement overall. This was done to drive accountability and to create a healthy sense of competition among their extended leadership team.

To understand how well they were doing and to assess the impact made through market unit and functional action plans, they ran a pulse survey. This also collected qualitative feedback in order to gauge how well people had been involved in local action planning around the organisation.

In the next full "Our Way, Our Voice" survey, a year later, there had been a significant positive shift in engagement and indeed the climate across the organisation.

People were more favourable about their opportunities for personal development, many more people believed information was being shared effectively, and leadership scores were up on all questions, but particularly in terms of agility, speed and acting as one company.

The overall result was that trust and confidence was much higher. Most people were optimistic – believing that things will continue to change for the better.

Looking back on the progress they had made, some of the key success factors included identifying a small number of key priorities, targeting action planning, tapping into the creative power of human networks, and establishing clear accountability.

According to Tim, "There is much more sense of us being Nomad Foods now. There are still some barriers to break down and there are still some old legacy ways of working, but we have made huge progress. People talk about "Our Way, Our Voice". We are moving on from doing the basics to really bringing our values to life."

Improving engagement on the railways: Merseyrail

If it is hard to create high levels of engagement in factories, the engagement challenges in the rail sector in the UK are even more considerable. (As someone who has worked with more than a dozen train operating companies over the years – while also being a commuter – I am being very polite here).

The franchise system, which awards the operation of passenger services to private operators, remains controversial. There are strong unions and poor industrial relations. Passenger satisfaction is low. There is a lot of service disruption, in part due to a major upgrade of the network. Passenger numbers have doubled over the last twenty years and Britain's railway network is the most congested in Europe. Front-line staff, of course, bear the brunt of passenger concerns. Personal safety at the gate-line and on trains is a major concern for staff.

In terms of employee engagement, compared to other industries, there are three main challenges in the rail sector: communication, customer focus and front-line management.

It is difficult to communicate effectively with hard-to-reach groups like drivers. Generally, these employees are detached from company goals. There is relatively low pride. Drivers identify with the industry as much as their employer. The tenure of drivers and other rail staff can be quite high, meaning it can cover a longer period than just the most recent franchise. In other words, many drivers have potentially seen several train operating companies come and go over the years, and have out-survived them all.

There is a lot of scepticism about customer focus in the sector. Relatively few rail staff believe their company truly cares about passengers, for example. Here the rail industry is below the transport sector as a whole. Staff can be dealing with customers affected by problems beyond their control and sometimes without the information they need to communicate with passengers clearly. This leads to a lot of frustration.

Across the sector, there are low scores on manager effectiveness, especially feedback and recognition. This indicates a challenge in recruiting and developing effective front-line leaders across the industry. Typically, the industry prioritises delivery and task focus over good people management.

One company that has managed to improve engagement, despite these challenges is Merseyrail.

Merseyrail is the commuter metro rail service for Liverpool and the surrounding area. It is a joint venture between Serco and Abellio, who were awarded a 25-year concession agreement in 2003.

It operates over 600 services per day to 68 stations throughout the Liverpool City Region, including 4 underground stations in the city centre that receive services every few minutes. The network carries over 100,000 passengers on an average weekday, with Liverpool Central station being one of the busiest outside of London. The company has 1,200 employees, working in operations, engineering, customer service and head office roles.

Despite being one of the most punctual and reliable rail networks, it has faced its own workforce challenges. These included a strike over future plans for driver-only operated trains. This relates to the introduction of a new fleet, which is greatly needed as the company had some of the oldest rolling stock in the UK.

There is also an investment in the network (stations, signalling and track), but these upgrades can sometimes cause delays, which leads to frustration for passengers and staff alike.

As a result of these problems, scores in their annual engagement survey fell, particularly on questions relating to how people feel about the company's values and principles. The sharpest fall was amongst operations staff (train crew).

So leaders redoubled their efforts at communicating with these hard-to-reach groups and addressing employee concerns.

Their companywide action plan focused on improving leader visibility, especially during periods of disruption. This included introducing monthly update videos from the Managing Director, Andy Heath, which were short and easy-to-access. The videos allow more direct and personal communications, which are delivered digitally and in a timelier manner.

The company introduced an innovation platform called "Help ME" where managers are able to post about a business problem or simply ask staff for their input and ideas. This was designed to increase involvement and to tap into the experience of employees. Every staff member across the business has the opportunity to provide their input. Again, this was a more transparent and digital way of involving and communicating with people.

Related to this focus on continuous improvement, the company set up a business-wide working group, which they called an Acceleration Squad. Staff members volunteered to join the group which looked at ways to increase revenue. The squad included members from all levels and grades across the business. It was another attempt to tap into the collective insights of employees.

It's worth noting that none of these focus areas could be described as soft or HR issues. Employee engagement at Merseyrail is seen as a business improvement activity. Engagement can be tied to passenger feedback and to safety and operational performance. Leaders can improve these outcomes by involving people in fixing problems and finding solutions, and by supporting them to do so.

The HR team also invested in better digital tools and mobile apps for communicating their benefits programme to employees. Their new portal consolidated their existing benefits into on easy-to-access tool. This led to greater awareness of and uptake of key benefits. They also introduced spot awards as a way of recognising staff achievements with small gift cards.

Their engagement survey also led to specific departmental actions that they tracked progress on. All functions had their own plan, but the greatest focus (and the greatest number of actions) was in their operations team.

As a result of this effort, scores rebounded strongly in their next engagement survey. The biggest improvements related to confidence in senior managers' decisions and feeling that the company involves people and treats people with respect (in accordance with their values).

The pride that people say they have in the company increased by 17 percentage points. In operations, one-in-four people were more positive about the way the company lives its values and principles.

This is a huge shift for any organisation in a year. It indicates the progress that can be made, even during periods of change and uncertainty, when engagement is tied to business improvement, staff are involved in making changes, and when a focus on values is role-modelled from the top.

Improving call centre engagement at Esure

Call centres also present specific challenges for organisational leadership.

Call centres are human capital intensive, with people accounting for approximately 70 per cent of their operating costs. In addition to head count, another human cost inherent in call centre operations is higher-than-average employee turnover. Call centre agents have shorter average job tenures than employees in other organisations, with many call centre employees leaving within just two years of joining. The demanding nature of call centre environments contribute to the high turnover. Among the challenges workers face are frequently-shifting priorities and workloads, and working with many different internal processes.

One company that has used employee surveys to transform the culture in its call centres is the insurance company esure.

Esure was founded in 2000 by its chairman Sir Peter Wood. Sir Peter is a direct-selling pioneer. He understood the potential of direct-selling insurance over the telephone 15 years earlier, with the launch of Direct Line. At the turn of the millennium he set his sights on the potential of the internet, with his aim to streamline the process of buying car and home insurance.

Within five years, esure became one of the fastest growing UK insurers ever, receiving awards for its cover, online services and creative marketing. The company now has over 1,500 employees. Its head office is in Surrey. Its call centres are in Manchester and Glasgow.

I started working with esure in 2015. Up to that point, the focus of HR had been on managing the company's fast growth and putting out fires. Under a new head of HR, Helen Taylor, the organisation had reached a stage in its evolution where it needed to focus on building more of a high performance culture. There was also a need to reduce employee turnover in its call centres.

The first survey showed the work that needed to be done. For call centre employees, engagement was low. There was a concern over work processes. People did not get much one-on-one time with their team leader. Some of the factors specifically affecting turnover included pay, limited chances for progression, inflexible shift patterns, and inadequate communication of changes to things like scripts and processes. There was a general sense of feeling undervalued. They were a difficult set of survey results for a company that prided itself on great service and being nimble.

Over the next twelve months, the company fixed some of the foundational issues. For example, they implemented a new simplified grading structure and introduced a revised pay framework. They appointed a Learning and Development Manager and a Head of Communications.

They also tackled some quick wins. These included allowing people to have drinks at their desks. They introduced WIFI in their canteens (important for a young workforce). They relaxed the dress code. Up to this point, as you can tell, they had been quite a traditionally-managed and hierarchical organisation. These were important, visible changes to some of the established symbols of their culture.

In their second survey, only a few survey categories had inched upwards. It was clear to leaders that they needed to increase their efforts in key areas.

The CEO Stuart Vann embarked on a comprehensive series of all-colleague road shows in order to improve communications. They represented a new style of communications: direct, personal and open. He also spent time in call centres talking to staff and listening in to calls. This was a shock to the system – not only for employees on the phones, but also for their team leaders. Stuart started a series of CEO Business Updates, keeping all colleagues informed on key business news. The company also invested in training 120 managers, putting them through Leader Communication workshops that were designed to improve local dialogue.

The investment in leadership also included a Management Excellence Programme for 100 team leaders. This involved seven days of development time per participant over an 18-month period. They launched their first Future Leaders Programme and a new Rising Stars Programme for employees. These were reinforced by a new esure Leadership Framework, which set out clear standards and behaviours for the first time.

These actions were about building organisational capability and transforming the culture of the workplace. The change was driven from the top. Interventions were made across all levels of the organisation.

The results were impressive. In their third employee survey, leadership scores were up by 14 percentage points, communication scores by 16 points, and engagement by 8 points. From where they started, one quarter of the company was now more positive about communications – a fundamental shift.

There were also positive results in terms of attrition. Over this period, the turnover rate fell significantly. In the survey itself, the declared intention to leave also improved (in other words, fewer people stated they intended to leave). In 2015, over half of employees in the survey indicated they might consider leaving the company. Three years later, that figure was down to a third.

Esure's story shows the great progress that can be made when engagement is considered as part of an overall culture change.

The company also used people analytics to track cohorts. This included "The class of 2015" which had 276 new starters in it – mainly people in their early 20s. They tracked the change in engagement in this class through a series of pulse surveys. When they looked at the primary reasons for leaving, given by people during exit surveys, they were lifestyle changes and other career opportunities, rather than being unhappy with the culture or unsatisfied with their manager. This is the kind of integrated analytics that is discussed in more detail in the later chapter on employee experience.

How to run an effective engagement survey

These examples show how some companies have successfully used employee surveys to create meaningful and positive change. But that's not always the case. It is hard work to run them as well as these three companies do. As a result, it has become fashionable to criticise engagement surveys. This criticism mirrors that of other important management routines, like performance reviews, which are also hard to do well.

I highlight some of the problems with employee engagement in the next chapter. In many cases, the criticism of employee surveys is probably fair. I regularly encounter companies who struggle to get value from their surveys, especially those that are run through pure technology solutions or those that are designed to win a place on a good employers' list.

In the rest of this chapter, though, I want to highlight the key ingredients that lead to an effective engagement survey process, of which there are also many examples.

Based on my experience there are five key success factors, which are survey-specific. In addition, there is an overall mindset that is necessary for success, one which regards engagement surveys as a means to drive culture change and organisational transformation.

Concrete objectives

The first survey success factor is obvious, but it's worth stating. It is being clear on what you're measuring and why. When I talk to companies that are running ineffective surveys, it is often because they have bought an off-the-shelf survey product or technology and they haven't clarified their research questions and overall goals beyond attaining an engagement score.

Any effective survey begins with stakeholder discussions to clarify the main goals, to ensure buy-in from leaders and other groups like works councils, and to refine content. There needs to be an effort to make questions as business relevant and specific as possible. It's also essential to begin with the ends in mind. When you get the results, what are the two or three business questions you want to answer?

To build on this point, even before thinking about a survey, you should start with the available evidence that already exists.

This is a key part of evidence-based management (there is more about this in the next chapter). Evidence can include data and insights from focus groups, informal discussions, other surveys you run, materials written on internal and external social media like Glassdoor, and so on. It may also include other organisational data, such as referral rates, performance feedback and turnover data. In addition, it can include a review of the general research and literature, for example on Research Gate or in publications like Harvard Business Review. In order to set clear objectives, the more you can narrow your focus, the more success you will have.

Accountability

The second success factor is accountability. You need to be clear from the outset who will be responsible for acting on the results, and by when. This is a key part of driving organisational transformation, as described in more detail shortly. More specifically, it also affects the questions you ask and how you clarify them.

In any large organisation, there are too many management layers and groups to ask about, and it's not a good idea to simply ask the same question over and over about different levels. For example, in order to explore communications, you could ask how colleagues share information within your team; how your manager communicates with you; how you hear about what's going on in your function, business unit, country, division, and the company as a whole. This is simply too repetitious, so you need to decide who will be responsible for taking action on the results and what you will ask about them specifically. Where do you think you have communication gaps?

Ideally, your answer to that question comes from good evidence. In any organisation you can review performance data to understand the key leverage points for driving success.

In a retail network, for example, it is often the area manager that is the key leverage point, driving success at both branch and region levels. In this case, you might want to ask a number of questions about the effectiveness of your area managers and few if any questions about region managers. The role of region managers in your engagement survey, in this situation, is to support and coordinate action planning at the area manager level, rather than to directly take action on region-level results themselves.

One way you can put specific groups on the hook for taking action on the results is by using clear definitions. In a survey, it's typical to provide a list of key terms. Best practice is to be as specific as possible. If I ask any questions about an executive team, for example, I usually list the executives' names, rather than have a general description. Not only does this act as a form of downward communication, it leaves no wriggle room when it comes to debating the results with that executive team.

Specificity

The use of survey definitions also relates to the third success factor, which is to be as clear and specific as possible in all areas. This includes communicating how the results will be used, by whom, and when. It means using survey instructions that explain how individual responses are anonymised. It includes the survey questions themselves. You need to avoid questions that are wordy, jargon-y or vague. It's important to avoid double-barrelled questions. Do not use questions that lead respondents towards a preferred response.

The most practical way to ensure a survey is efficient, clear and specific is to test it. This typically means a couple of employee focus groups in different work environments and locations. As well as getting feedback on the questions, it's a means of softly communicating about the survey and involving people in the process.

When it comes to questionnaire design, it's important to think of outcomes and enablers. Some questions need to measure outcomes, such as pride and satisfaction. These are not areas you can take action on directly, so other questions should be designed to measure the behaviours that impact those outcomes. By using a key driver analysis (a regression with, for example, pride as the dependent variable) you can prioritise behaviours in terms of their impact (for example, through a dominance analysis).

It's also important to separate your outcome variables. For example, retention (often measured by someone's declared intention to stay or leave the organisation) is best analysed separately to pride or satisfaction. This is because "intention to stay/leave" often has different drivers, usually more related to hygiene factors. Too often, I see engagement scores that are a poor mix of various outcome and enabler items. In these cases "engagement" is just an "overall average" (and I can guess that the score is likely to be a pretty meaningless 70 per cent).

This is a common criticism of an engagement model like "Say, Stay, Strive." The "Stay" element – peoples' intention to stay at the organisation – shouldn't be combined with "Say" (advocacy) and "Strive (discretionary effort). For example, you can get improving engagement index scores simply because of a general economic downturn and a subsequent reduction of job opportunities elsewhere. In other words, not due to anything you have done. You may in fact have a serious problem, because employees with low pride and low energy are actually trapped in place, unable to move on.

Another element to consider is question order. It's best to mix questions up rather than organise them by topic. Generally, it's advisable to start with easier questions and leave harder ones to later. What's most important is to keep a similar philosophy to question ordering across your surveys and over time.

Another way to keep surveys efficient is to include a small number of follow-up questions. You can only ask follow-up questions two or three times in total. If used more than that, respondents realise they add to the completion time, and this can affect how they respond to the remainder of the survey. But follow-up items can be very useful. For example, someone rating their last performance review as "not helpful" can be asked for feedback on why.

Transparency

The fourth success factor is maximum transparency. As we saw earlier in this book with Google's listening strategy, transparency is a key part of a high-trust culture. For this reason, transparency and openness need to run through all aspects of an effective engagement survey programme. This includes communications about objectives, respondent anonymity, data management, results analysis and action planning.

One way to help with transparency is to keep things simple. This includes having overall objectives that are aligned to business priorities. It means making it clear how you keep responses safe.

It also refers to the reporting back of the results. Often, when I come across a company running an ineffective engagement survey, it's because managers don't understand the maths used to report the results. This can be due to using an unusual response scale. People also struggle with mean scores and calculations like a score out of a thousand or even a NPS number. My rule of thumb is, if you have to explain the maths, there's a problem.

Keeping things simple extends to how you communicate the results. Dashboards are good, but managers should also get access to all the relevant results. Overly-fancy visualisations are often a diversion. The ability to judge a score relative to trend or internal and external benchmarks is useful in terms of accounting for bias. Having a way of identifying statistically significant differences is also useful, especially for the results of small teams. In a group of ten, one person accounts for a 10 per cent swing. That may look dramatic, but it isn't. Testing for significance can help clarify this.

Triangulation and sense-making

The fifth success factor is triangulation. In social science research, this means validating results by cross verification from two or more sources. Ideally, a combination of research methods, for example, quantitative and qualitative.

My recommendation is that when it comes to employee survey results analysis, you should be using as many different data sources as possible and integrating their combined findings into a discussion about what they're telling you.

First, there are the overall survey results. You can apply multiple lenses to these, including trend data (if available) and certainly internal and external benchmarks. These can help you identify any unusual patterns that are the result of recent changes or internal factors.

You can also examine the internal variation in scores by unit, location, function, job level, length of service and demographics. It's important to understand the range of scores in order to judge consistency. You can identify bright spots and hot spots. There are advanced analytics you can use, such as classification trees and segmentation.

Second, there are the open-ended comments you collect. It can be a frustrating experience to complete any survey if there is no space for you to express your views freely. So in most cases, an employee engagement survey includes space for free-text comments at the end. The more specific and constructive the open question is, the better results it will yield. (Simply providing open space will produce a predictable list of complaints.) You can code the comments responses and use techniques like natural language processing (which is discussed in more depth later).

I always recommend that clients look at the comments second. In other words, that they begin with the quantitative data. This is because certain comments can be very powerful and persuasive, even though they only represent an individual's point of view.

It's better to explore specific questions when looking at the qualitative data, such as why is our performance review system not seen as helpful? Or why are corporate communications not getting through to the shop floor? Using comments in this way is akin to running an instant focus group.

Third, there are other data points you can bring to the analysis. These include the results of other surveys, focus group feedback, and input collected informally on site visits or during town hall meetings.

There are also the data that sit on internal social media (Workplace, Yammer, and so on) and on external social media (like Glassdoor, LinkedIn and even Twitter). Other data may also be available, such as feedback from recruiters and from recent hires or departures.

The other critical point of triangulation is, of course, business performance. Do engagement scores correlate with actual business performance as measured by sales, productivity, safety, customer or other key results? If they do not, why not?

If there is a disconnect between business performance and engagement, it can be a powerful indicator of where that particular

85

organisation is in the change curve. For example, a unit with high engagement, but poor business results may well be operating in a silo. You would want to explore what's being communicated by local leadership. I have heard this kind of situation described as a "happy valley" (or more politely "pre-transition"). Conversely, in a unit with strong performance, but low engagement, you might question how those results are being achieved and wonder about their sustainability.

By integrating these different sources, you can develop a deeper understanding of your employee engagement scores. But the other essential ingredient in this process is time, especially time for sense-making. Leaders now have the ability to review engagement survey results immediately. But to get the most out of them it's essential to still build in time for review, reflection, interpretation and validation before taking action.

Change leadership

The five factors described above (clear objectives, specificity, accountability, transparency and triangulation) are key ingredients in running a successful employee engagement survey. Employee surveys are often criticised because these things are hard to do well. Without them, engagement efforts often fall at the first hurdle: the survey itself.

However, I would argue that the biggest barrier to a successful employee engagement programme is not the survey, but the mindset of those leading it. Any successful survey needs to be seen as part of an overall business transformation. A change leadership mindset needs to run through all elements.

This begins with senior leadership sponsorship. In companies that run engagement surveys well, senior leaders are involved in all stages and act as champions. They are committed to using the results and consider employee engagement an important leadership routine.

In driving change in any organisation, leadership is key. What does effective change leadership look like? There are three key components.

Firstly, effective change leaders build confidence. They do this through clear and direct communications, and by role-modelling the behaviours that are required, such as transparency and accountability. They set a small number of priorities, which they repeat over and over when they communicate. They ensure a focus on achieving them by removing potential obstacles and by providing sufficient resources.

Secondly, they help people answer the question, "What do I need to do differently?" They translate things into specific behaviours and give easy-to-understand examples. They recognise people, when they see those behaviours being practiced. They call it out when they see old ways of working still being followed.

Thirdly, they make things measurable. They set clear and tangible goals. This includes measures of effectiveness, such as participation, as well as measures of impact. Impact measures include both enablers (such as teamwork and collaboration) and outcomes (such as team performance and productivity). They communicate as much fresh and relevant business information as possible. They help people understand how the business works and their role in contributing to that success.

How do you ensure leaders are champions of your engagement survey process? They should be involved in survey design and have authorship of some of the content. You can pique leaders' curiosity by getting them to anticipate the results. You can ensure the relevance of the findings by linking surveys scores to business performance. You can provide effective tracking of action planning by measuring progress. Critically, you can capture and share success stories from managers and peers who have used survey insights effectively.

HR also has a key role to play in ensuring an engagement programme is effective. HR is the steward of the process, in the same way that marketing is on point for providing insight on customer feedback.

HR's role is to be a facilitator and coach. Importantly, they're responsible for collecting and sharing success stories and best practice. HR staff (often business partners) also have a consulting role in using engagement insights to build organisational capability.

Dave Ulrich in his book *Victory Through Organisation* highlights the key role HR plays in building organisational, as well as individual capability: "The scope of HR has expanded. For decades human resources has primarily referred to talent and all the ways in which people are managed, including bringing the right people into an organisation, moving them through the organisation, administering their benefits and other "hygiene" issues, and appropriately moving them out of the organisation. In recent years, HR has expanded from a nearly exclusive focus on people and how individuals think, behave, and act to an additional emphasis on organisation."

For Ulrich, "An organisation focus examines workplace as much as workforce, work processes as much as people, organisation capabilities as well as individual competencies."

In all these areas employee insights are critical and engagement is an overall measure of their effectiveness.

The other success factor in a change leadership mindset is the ability to leverage existing management routines to the maximum, rather than creating new ones. For example, how can you use engagement insights in business planning, organisational design, performance management, talent reviews, and so on?

Rather than creating survey-specific initiatives, the most effective programmes make the most of processes that already exist and build on plans that have already been made.

This focus on leveraging existing routines also extends to how leaders set targets. Any employee engagement target should be aligned to the way that other business targets are set. This includes the mix of outcomes and enablers that are included, measures of effectiveness and impact, and the degree of stretch or ambition that's included.

This overall change-leadership mindset, and the survey-specific factors, are critical in ensuring an effective engagement programme.

As set out at the start of this chapter, most large companies currently run some kind of engagement survey and have done so for a number of years. The next chapter reflects on some of the problems with employee engagement. These are part of the reason why some companies are exploring new approaches to employee listening. But it's not only companies who struggle with engagement who are looking at doing things differently. It includes companies who currently do a good job with their engagement programmes, as described above. They realise there are new opportunities to do more and to build trust more effectively. They are starting to move beyond employee engagement by adopting a focus on employee experience.

6. Beyond Engagement

In my career, I have been able to look closely at companies that have peaked and fallen and maybe risen again, including the likes of Blackberry, IBM and Nokia. I am fascinated by the ability of some companies to reinvent themselves, while others do not.

I believe the best leaders always view employee insights in terms of a story about transformation. They use employee feedback to understand where people are in the change curve. They use that intelligence to navigate change more effectively.

The economist Joseph Schumpeter is famous for studying business cycles. Schumpeter is associated with phrase "creative destruction" which describes how entrepreneurship and innovation are disruptive forces that sustain economic growth by destroying the value of long-established companies and monopolies.

In his 1942 book, *Capitalism, Socialism and Democracy*, which is obviously a product of its tumultuous time, he wrote: "The opening up of new markets and the organisational development from the craft shop and factory to such concerns as US Steel illustrate the process of industrial mutation that incessantly revolutionises the economic structure from within, incessantly destroying the old one, incessantly creating a new one ... [The process] must be seen in its role in the perennial gale of creative destruction."

That evocative phrase has always struck me, "the perennial gale". This book takes the long-view on what's happening in the world of employee insights, the field I have worked in for the last 20 years. During only those two decades the employee survey industry provides an almost perfect microcosm of what has happened more generally in the economy.

It has moved from a mostly analogue world to a digital one. It has been globalised. Small entrepreneurs have sold their firms to multinational behemoths. The whole sector is being transformed anew by mobile technologies and big data.

It's a delicious irony to me that a field which studies disruption and change is itself being hugely disrupted, facing its own winds of change.

Let's begin by looking at some of the reasons why we got here.

Marketing employee engagement

In many ways, the employee engagement industry is an incredible success story. It has grown into a global multi-billion dollar industry, employing thousands of people. Engagement is an important topic for leaders, government and regulators. It has become an umbrella term for a wide range of consulting and technology services, having grown out of a fairly small and specialised employee research sector.

One reason for this growth is that employee engagement is a great term from a marketing perspective. It makes a direct emotional appeal and references the promise that exists at the heart of the employment deal. This is what Bill Kahn intended when he first used the term in 1990. Gallup then popularised engagement surveys and through its global marketing reach created a huge impact.

Engagement was an easy concept for many business leaders to understand, in contrast to many of the other terms HR colleagues used. The economy had shifted towards a greater emphasis on knowledge work, and this effort is harder to measure than, for example, manufacturing productivity and working hours. So the intangible value of "going the extra mile" and of winning employees' discretionary effort was understood to be increasingly important.

In fact, employee engagement is one of the few HR measures that business leaders have really bought into. Jack Welch, the successful long-term CEO of GE, for example, remarked that, "There are only three measurements that tell you nearly everything you need to know about your organisation's overall performance: employee engagement, customer satisfaction, and cash flow... It goes without saying that no company, small or large, can win over the long run without energized employees who believe in the mission and understand how to achieve it."

HR has been glad to have something that leaders bought into at a time when the value of the function was frequently challenged. As technology made it easier to deal with traditional resourcing and personnel issues, HR has looked for a more strategic role to play as a true business partner. Employee engagement gave HR a reason for having a seat at the top table.

A survey of chief executives by The Conference Board in 2014 found that "raising employee engagement" was a top priority for CEOs in every region of the world, placed above improving performance management, enhancing leadership development and improving front-line management.

Defining engagement

The employee engagement industry has happily floated on this tide of interest. But there are problems lurking below.

For example, although it is clearly related to earlier work on satisfaction and commitment, engagement itself does not have a lot of academic research to back it up. It doesn't even have a commonly-agreed definition.

In 2008, the UK Government established a task force to look into employee engagement, which was led by David MacLeod (a former colleague) and Nita Clarke. In the course of producing their report, called *Engaging for Success*, they identified 50 different definitions of employee engagement, which often varied widely.

Rob Briner of the Centre for Evidence Based Management at the University of Bath wrote a blistering review of the employee engagement literature in 2014. He noted that, "Definitional problems are serious [and] measures of employee engagement a mess. They often consist of items from different and pre-existing surveys thrown together to form something apparently 'new'."

This has been useful for many engagement survey providers, who have packaged and sold their own flavour of engagement model, but it has created a problem for those looking to introduce standards. It's one reason why so many companies measure employee engagement in so many different ways.

I have come across more than a dozen methods for producing an engagement score (and I am sure many more methods exist that I have not encountered). These include a number out of a thousand, a mean score out of five or ten, the percentage of people responding the same way across several items, the percentage of people with a mean score over a certain amount to an index of questions, a net promoter-style score which can be positive or negative, and so on.

The fact that different engagement providers measure things in different ways makes it hard for a company to switch vendors. If they want to continue to measure their trend in employee engagement, they are potentially locked into a proprietary approach.

It is also a struggle for any investor who wants to understand the value of a company's intangible, human-capital assets, when there are so many alternative ways of reporting on engagement.

Without singling them out, Gallup's own story is reflective of these issues.

The questions used in Gallup's 12-item survey – whose publication, remember, was the catalyst for so much of the subsequent focus on engagement – actually read like a traditional team climate survey. The questions don't feel very different from anything that preceded them. The twelve questions measure local work experience factors such as clear job expectations, having the materials and equipment you need, and receiving recognition and praise.

Gallup's own scoring approach is also pretty opaque. They do not really disclose how they separate "engaged" from "not engaged" or "actively disengaged" employees. They present mean scores for their survey questions and an overall "Grand Mean". Presumably the "engaged" figure comes from the percentage of people who respond a certain way to a combination of their items.

The convenient effect of this approach is that it produces a low score for the per cent who are "engaged". This creates handily dramatic headlines for its State of the Global Workplace Reports. But when they say (as they did in 2017) that "only 10 per cent of employees in Western Europe are engaged in their work," it generally feels like marketing has overtaken common sense.

Given these measurement issues, it's perhaps surprising that it has become commonplace to accept that engagement has an important impact on business performance. Some people have done great research linking engagement to performance measures, such as customer satisfaction, sales performance, safety and efficiency measures. But the best of that research is client-specific (and unpublished). Many general (published) studies have looked at correlations or have relied heavily on anecdotes. Some of the general evidence appears to suffer from the "halo effect". As described by Phil Rosenzweig, this means succumbing to "the delusion of connecting the winning dots by only looking at successful companies and finding their common features."

Recently, people have also started to wonder how much of engagement is actually just down to personality. A meta-analysis in 2018, by Henry Young et al, of 114 different survey samples, looked to estimate the degree to which people differed in their level of engagement because of their individual character traits.

The study found that 48 per cent of the variability in engagement could be predicted by people's personality. In particular, four traits were important: positive affectivity (in other words, cheerfulness and enthusiasm), proactivity, conscientiousness and extroversion.

Obviously, job-related and other organisational factors are still critical in employee engagement, but the research raises the question of whether companies can simply hire for engagement instead of having to build it? I am not going to go into the difficulties of assessing potential candidates for these traits here, but the research highlights the important individual dimension to employee engagement, which is sometimes overlooked when defining what it means.

Problems with engagement

Despite some of these concerns, engagement has been well marketed and it has been generally well received. It has clearly hit a nerve.

Twenty years ago, I had to spend time persuading leaders to invest in efforts to listen to their employees. It was not clear to many executives why this was a useful thing to do. That is certainly not the case any longer. Nearly all large organisations now have employee engagement programmes. Most companies make a significant investment in employee listening. For many companies their engagement survey has become a routine.

I now spend my time having a different kind of discussion with leaders, which is to do something better with their investment in employee listening than their current programme. This is because there can be downsides to a focus on employee engagement.

For one thing, prioritising employee engagement over and above everything else has led to a dumbing down of employee research. Companies sometimes fail to try to answer their most important business questions through employee research, opting for a default approach instead.

For another, there is a dark side to the focus on engagement. In essence, always going the extra mile is just not sustainable. Leaders should be aware of the problems caused by the acceleration trap.

There is also an overall concern about the focus on engagement for engagement's sake.

Let's look at these downsides in more detail, before discussing how the industry is now being transformed and how many companies are now starting to move beyond engagement.

The dumbing down of employee research

For most of the history of employee surveys, work has been driven by new thinking and approaches coming out of behavioural science. We have already traced the development of work in sociology and psychology that influenced early employee surveys, for example, from morale and climate, to job satisfaction and commitment. Early employee surveys applied and tested new management approaches, from motivation theory to participative management systems.

In this period, survey content was tailored and customised to a company's specific needs and business priorities. In fact, through stakeholder involvement, business leaders were often co-creators of the surveys. HR's role was sometimes minimal.

Customisation meant that surveys could be used to answer specific business questions. Insights from employees about the climate within the organisation could help leaders identify and fix important problems. These might relate to topics such as embedding your business strategy, building greater customer service orientation, removing obstacles to innovation, and so on.

As such, these surveys were a form of direct upward consulting to CEOs and leaders. The early employee survey firms certainly saw themselves as making up a uniquely objective upward-consulting profession. The founders felt they were diagnosticians, taking an x-ray of a body corporate. They gave a voice to the rank and file. Consequently, they had a duty of care in presenting those voices truthfully and honestly at board level.

To some extent, they were helping institute a Third Way model of corporate governance, an idea that was very popular at the time in both the UK and the USA. Surveys were a direct channel to the workforce that operated outside of traditional – sometimes hostile – union labour relations. At the same time, the use of surveys ensured that the views of workers were represented in management decision making.

Science, especially medical science, was a metaphor used by all the early employee survey firms. There is a kind of dignity in this. At the time, a survey was still a cutting edge tool for social science research. The contents of surveys reflected the best of academic thinking. Approaches were informed by theory. Questions were tailored and specific. There was a clear research question. Results were analysed with scientific rigour by experts back in the survey lab. The findings were revealed to senior leaders in a detached and objective fashion, often in great detail.

But there is also a coolness to this approach. The expert-client relationship can be a frustrating one. Problems that are identified remain with the client, as it's not the role of the diagnostician to fix things. Once the failings are pointed out, leaders need to take their own medicine. The survey expert will return in a year's time for your next check-up, to see how you're getting along. Hopefully you have improved or you will get a telling off.

Given that HR was just another stakeholder, there was also an important people dimension that could be lost from the discussion around solutions. In fact, HR could become frustrated that they were not more involved. They wanted to own (or facilitate the process of using) employee insights, just as the sales and marketing function owned customer insights.

So when Gallup launched their approach, things were ripe for change. Employee engagement, which did not originate in academia, but in the world of polling and packaged consulting, seemed to satisfy many of the frustrations which had been building up. This is a key reason for its explosive growth.

Employee engagement was simpler to understand and easier to implement. Engagement could also have the benefit of letting senior leaders off the hook, in terms of taking direct action. Undoubtedly, one great attraction of the Gallup approach for some executives, is that it focuses attention almost exclusively on the role of team leaders.

Gallup's research led to the well-worn phrase that "people leave managers not companies." I worry how much damage that short refrain has caused. It's simply too convenient for senior leaders to blame immediate managers for their workforce motivation problems. Moreover, it's plainly nonsense when in any large organisation front-line manager capability is only one piece of the organisational effectiveness jigsaw.

As engagement became a common business term, it led to commodification. The people leading engagement programmes needed experience in using the tools rather than a background in behavioural science. Because things were standardised, engagement solutions could be pre-packaged and added on. The most common engagement solution by far was manager training, which was something most companies probably needed to do anyway.

All of this was, of course, fuelled by technological changes that made the running of employee surveys easier, faster and cheaper. The frequency and cadence of surveys increased. An annual engagement survey was no longer enough. Companies needed to monitor engagement levels more frequently, just as they do with other business metrics. Even though this meant that the time for addressing root causes was squeezed.

In all this momentum, however, something was lost: the focus on making sure that you collected business-critical insights, not just engagement scores.

In the earlier employee survey era, there had been a link to both specific leadership priorities and the latest research in social science. Both connection points make employee research harder to do. But they are essential in providing insights that are fit for evidence-based management and decision making.

Evidence-based management

There is a growing interest in evidence-based management at the present time. Denise Rousseau, Rob Briner and Eric Barends of the Centre for Evidence Based Management define it as, "Making decisions through the conscientious, explicit and judicious use of the best available evidence from multiple sources."

This includes, "Translating a practical issue or problem into an answerable question, systematically searching for and retrieving the evidence, critically judging the trustworthiness and relevance of the evidence, weighing and pulling together the evidence, incorporating the evidence into the decision-making process and then evaluating the outcome of the decision taken to increase the likelihood of a favourable outcome."

A critical element is that before making an important decision, you ask "What is the available evidence?" and that you take into account the scientific literature and the concerns of those affected by decisions you make.

On the basis of these principles, Rob Briner concluded in 2014 that "engagement is more like a muddy puddle than clear water [and] HR needs to put the concept back under the microscope."

Of course, many companies have run excellent engagement surveys, which combine a focus on employee engagement with other important business issues, and that have led to meaningful, positive change. The examples in the previous chapter and elsewhere in this book highlight what's possible.

But that's not always the case. Sometimes employee engagement surveys are managed poorly. Their content is non-specific. They are dull to complete. They are repeated too frequently. They are done for appearances sake or to get on a best places list, rather than to truly improve organisational effectiveness. Worst of all is when there is a lack of critical thinking about what is being measured and why.

How bad is the problem? In a recent study, only 48 per cent of senior managers said they believe their company's engagement survey is highly valuable. Worryingly, the score was much lower for front-line employees (just 19 per cent).

These scores are in line with other studies that have been done, so the indications are that only around half of the employee engagement surveys that are run by companies are effective. Remember that most large companies run engagement surveys and they do so on at least an annual basis.

Sustainable engagement

There is another problem with engagement that gets at its core definition of "going the extra mile." Firstly, this is a phrase born out of US corporate culture and it does not translate well into some other work cultures. Secondly, there is an issue with the sustainability of always going the extra mile. This has become especially clear in recent years.

The 2008 financial crisis was a key moment in the modern history of many corporations. The Great Recession that followed has had a profound impact on the use of resources and on organisational design. In simple terms, every company has had do more with less.

Every organisation today is lean. Most companies are looking to use technology to become even leaner.

In the UK, overall business investment, which is a long-term challenge for the economy, fell sharply after 2008 (according to the Office for National Statistics). It only climbed back to pre-2008 levels in 2015, leaving behind a significant investment gap. It is a key reason for the weak productivity that has been a defining trend of the UK economy since 2008.

The use of temporary, freelance or independent workers has also risen since 2008. The number of self-employed workers increased rapidly immediately after the 2008 crash and the number of new full-time employees only caught up with the growth in self-employed workers at the end of 2014. Within the ranks of the self-employed, around 1.3 million are freelancers (making up around 4 per cent of the working population in the UK). Many freelancers operate in the "gig economy" – in other words operating on temporary contracts or piece work.

So companies are doing more with less, through a different mix of employees and other (often less secure) worker types, whilst coping with an investment shortfall. At the same time, digital technologies have ushered waves of transformation and change and led to a demand for new skills.

Every business I know is reworking its core processes and implementing new systems. This includes new enterprise management systems, new HR information systems, new customer relationship management systems, and so on.

Most functions are going through some kind of digital transformation. This creates significant pressures on organisations and individuals who are often managing the introduction of complex new systems at the same time as keeping legacy systems and existing processes running smoothly. Change programmes typically add to people's workload, especially in the short-to-medium-term.

Another side effect of digital transformation has been the rise of instantaneous communication and "always on" work culture. For employees in global functions the work day can easily flow across time zones. In London, this might mean an early start with colleagues in Asia, a full working day, followed by evening meetings and catch-ups with colleagues in the US.

The traditional boundaries of working days or weekends can be blurred and eroded, especially as people's expectations regarding accessibility and speed of response also ratchet up.

All of these elements mean that always going the extra mile can have harmful consequences.

Heike Bruch and Joechen Menges describe this situation as "the acceleration trap". Faced with the pressures described here, and new and intense competition, corporations often take on more than they can handle: "They increase the number and speed of their activities, raise performance goals, shorten innovation cycles, and introduce new management technologies or organisational systems. For a while, they succeed brilliantly, but too often the CEO tries to make this furious pace the new normal. What began as an exceptional burst of achievement becomes chronic overloading with dire consequences. Not only does the frenetic pace sap employee motivation, but the company's focus is scattered in various directions, which can confuse customers and threaten the brand."

This notion of an acceleration trap is very real and common. You need strict discipline and a razor-sharp focus in order to avoid it (and to break out of it when it becomes critical). Bruch and Menges suggest strategies such as forcibly halting less-important work and prioritising only a few must-win projects.

The human costs of the acceleration trap are widespread. In the UK, according to the Health and Safety Executive, 12.5 million working days were lost to work-related stress, depression or anxiety in 2017. That figure involves around half a million workers. This number has been consistent (with only small fluctuations) since the financial crash. The top causes, according to the HSE Labour Force Survey, are workload and lack of support.

Interestingly, rates of work-related stress, depression or anxiety are worst in large-size workforces. It's in large companies where the acceleration trap is most prevalent and where the complicatedness of getting work done is felt most sharply.

Stress is also more acute in some sectors than others. In the technology sector it can be especially problematic. The co-founder of Reddit, Alexis Ohanian, recently warned about the acceleration trap in the tech sector, which he characteristically renamed "hustle porn": "Hustle porn is one of the most toxic, dangerous things in the tech industry right now. And I know so much of it comes from the States. It is this idea that unless you are suffering, unless you are grinding, unless you are working every hour of every day and posting about it on Instagram, you're not working hard enough."

As a result of these pressures and the human cost, many organisations have realised that there is a danger in viewing engagement solely in terms of going the extra mile.

Engagement efforts are more effective when they are run in combination with a focus on employee well-being. This includes proactive health and wellness programmes, access to healthcare and mental health support. It includes having a healthy and safe physical work environment. It also means creating work-schedule and working-place flexibility.

Sustainable engagement results from both high pride and feeling you are able to sustain your level of performance over time, without being burnt out on the acceleration trap.

There are two other critical elements to truly sustainable engagement. One is a focus on enabling people to perform their best work. In part, this is about the way people work, ensuring people have the time, space and responsibility they need to do their job well.

It also means focusing on the tools, software and systems people use. Delays, slow connections, crash-outs, inefficient processes and so on, are all derailers of performance. They create huge amounts of frustration, especially when people know they have to work fast and smart in order to get everything done.

The other element of sustainable engagement is ensuring that teams benefit from inclusion and diversity. This includes diversity of background and experiences, diversity of thinking and attitudes, and diversity in ways of tacking work problems.

There is a lot of research that connects inclusion and diversity to improved performance. Scott Page, for example, highlighted the importance of diversity of perspectives on team performance in his 2008 book *The Difference*. In particular, he highlighted how innovation depends on diverse people working together and by capitalising on their individuality. This is an essential human performance element of sustainable engagement.

These connections to well-being, enablement and inclusion are critical in order to avoid the acceleration trap and to create sustainable engagement, rather than simply focusing on extra-effort and running faster.

They also highlight the need to view engagement more holistically than in the narrow confines of always going above and beyond. This more holistic perspective, as explained in the next chapter, is often referred to as employee experience, and at its heart is the goal of creating more human-centred workplaces.

What is unique and special about engagement?

Many of the problems with employee engagement come from a narrow focus on engagement for the sake of measuring engagement. Too often, engagement is just seen as a score. The score indicates whether people are investing enough individual effort. In this situation, engagement isn't put into a broader strategic context.

However, not all companies have made this mistake. In fact, many organisations have managed to make great progress by building effective employee engagement programmes. They have found that focusing on engagement has led to more traction than previous efforts at measuring satisfaction and commitment did. Additionally, engagement is a great fit for the prevailing emphasis that many leaders place on intangible assets and human capital.

So what is it that engagement provides that is truly unique and special and which has struck such a chord?

The strongest aspect of employee engagement is that it measures the emotional attachment that employees have to their employer (their affective commitment). This is often measured through pride and advocacy – whether someone is willing to recommend the company as a good place to work.

This affective connection reflects the bond that exists between employee and employer. It provides a proxy measure for how well the employment deal (or employment value proposition) is articulated, understood and delivered. As such, it moves beyond traditional measures of job satisfaction, which tend to reflect hygiene factors, such as pay, benefits and a sense of fairness. Engagement is about the sense of connectedness that people want and get from their work.

The employment deal was discussed earlier in this book and is used here synonymously with employment value proposition. It refers to how companies articulate both the formal elements (pay, benefits, working hours, and so on) and the psychological contract (culture, purpose, impact, opportunity, and so on). Both are inherent in any employment relationship, including people who are not full-time employees.

In all organisations, the core tenets of the employment deal are in flux, but the proposition that is offered now is vastly different from the one which preceded it. The traditional deal emphasised loyalty and attentiveness, and it provided a set of rewards to match. These included promotions based on longevity and benefits that recognised long service. In today's lean organisations, which prize flexible working relationships and cost- and risk-management above all, loyalty has been replaced by identity and affiliation.

More important than longevity now is cultural fit and buy-in to the organisation's values. In this way, the right people can settle in easily and quickly make a contribution. That contribution may be immediate, but high impact. It doesn't need to be spread out over a long career.

As explained earlier in this book, the establishment of trust needs to be swift. Attentiveness and experience, which are managerial-type competencies, are now valued less than the ability to hit the ground running, critical technical skills, service orientation, creativity, innovation, experimentation and problem-solving.

Rather than discretionary effort, therefore, it is the cognitive and affective connections between employee and employer that is the unique and special contribution engagement makes to organisational effectiveness and business performance.

As the economy has changed, so that it emphasises knowledge work and technology, and when people are working in virtual and often global teams, this alignment equation becomes more important.

Alignment to the goals and values of the organisation drives identification with the brand and fit. By really buying into an organisation's purpose and by understanding the business goals and your own contribution, employees get a sense of meaning, accomplishment and fulfilment.

These are the golden threads that connect employees and corporations in the modern economy and which are captured through measuring aspects like pride and advocacy.

One of the challenges for the employee engagement industry is that these key elements don't have to be measured through a survey (and certainly not through a survey alone). Pride and advocacy can be observed though direct behaviour, for example on social media or via referrals and other data points. It's a key reason why the employee insights industry is going through a period of disruption at the present time. Organisations are figuring out how much they can measure directly, without infringing privacy concerns, and how much they need to still capture through surveys.

The employee engagement industry is at an inflection point. Although many companies have managed to achieve a lot by using employee surveys, the various problems with employee engagement are leading many to re-think their approach.

At the same time, there are exciting new opportunities to do more creative employee research through new technologies, analytics and resources.

In the rest of this chapter, I will highlight some of these key industry changes and the challenges and opportunities that arise as a result.

New technologies

The most obvious technology change to the employee engagement industry is the plethora of mobile tools that now exist, which allow companies to collect feedback on an as-needed basis.

These are very similar to a host of tools and apps that are used in market research. Indeed, they often replicate market research methodologies like Net Promoter Scores and smiley faces.

As a result, many companies now run more frequent surveys, often quarterly or even monthly, rather than just once a year. Surveys are shorter in length. They normally contain a core of questions that are always asked and then questions that change each time.

It's not clear that these tools are helping to raise the game in employee research. They often measure even looser concepts than engagement, such as mood and sentiment.

They're not easy to create action plans from. If administered to a sample of employees, there can be questions over the usefulness or validity of the results.

Done well, they can be more fun than traditional surveys and fit in with other types of game-based communications. Done poorly, they can just add to a sense of survey fatigue.

A less visible, but more impactful change is in employee surveys using data that is integrated with HR Information Systems. As the quality of data in these systems has improved, integration provides the ability to do far richer analytics. Some of these are highlighted in the next chapter, including for example, cohort analysis, linkage research, persona-based segmentation and talent analytics.

Another important technological advance is in database design and management. This includes moving from relational databases, which are often a cumbersome table of IDs, towards graph-based methods that emphasise the importance of connections between entities. These can be a more accurate reflection of modern networked organisations and provide more opportunities for social network analysis.

There have also been vast improvements in data visualisation. Reports are provided as dashboards and results are displayed in real time. Delivered online, managers can explore key results, just as they do with other management information they receive. Most survey reports copy the look and feel of business information tools and use a standard dashboard-type interface.

However, the biggest technology change is social media which creates new opportunities for continuous listening and discussion.

Social platforms such as Workplace, Teams and Slack incorporate chat, email, video, calendars, appointments, notes and collaboration tools. They provide the means for continuous real-time data gathering and conversation. They allow for internal marketing that is based on analytics, personalisation and automation.

This is the focus of the next chapter and falls under the framework of performance marketing. A core component of this approach is creating the space for and observing real-time conversation, and using automated and continuous data collection and analytics.

Internal expertise and investment

The growth of interest in employee engagement has led to an investment in resources inside many large companies.

In the early period of employee research, surveys were often managed by third-party specialist agencies. This included all aspects of project management and even results reporting. There was no one person inside an organisation who owned employee surveys, except perhaps the HR director who typically had ultimate oversight and provided direction.

Now, there is typically a head of employee engagement whose role includes survey design and management, analytics, insights, as well as action planning, facilitation, coaching, communication and change management.

An important advantage of using internal resources is that the process and associated communications can fit better with other organisational priorities and challenges. There is often more customisation and tailoring of key messages as a result.

The fact that many companies have built internal capability has a couple of additional implications. Firstly, there is an in-built commitment to a particular approach and, given internal vested interests, there can be increased inertia and a reluctance to change and innovate.

Secondly, an internal team needs support in specific areas only, depending on their personal experience and expertise. The days of requiring comprehensive end-to-end support from an external provider are largely gone.

Thirdly, a head of employee engagement is increasingly looking for a technology solution that allows them to deliver their vision for employee engagement. In turn, this means that the engagement industry has focused on providing software-as-a-service. This often means the capability to run surveys and to analyse results through easy-to-use do-it-yourself tools.

The development of internal expertise on the client side parallels similar changes in market research and customer experience a decade earlier. Indeed, sometimes employee engagement fits within a customer experience function inside large companies.

More commonly, however, employee engagement fits into either a talent department within the HR function or a people analytics unit. The latter might combine employee engagement with human capital measurement, talent analytics, workforce planning and HR information management.

As argued in the next chapter, the next evolution for an employee engagement team is to become an employee experience function operating within an enterprise-wide analytics team.

From social science to data science

Another consequence of the internal specialisation in employee engagement is increased separation from academic research, behavioural science and theory. The early employee research firms were all closely connected to university sociology and psychology departments. That's not the case anymore and arguably this disconnect between academia and engagement practitioners has helped to limit innovation in the field.

This disconnect is also growing as practitioners move in the direction of data science approaches. These are also quite detached from social science theory.

It is actually quite hard to define what data science is. Vincent Granville, includes all the following categories of work in his definition of a data scientist: statisticians, mathematicians, data engineers, machine learning experts, software engineers, and visualisation experts.

According to Sean McClure, "Data science approaches are used to create models that capture the underlying patterns of complex systems, and codify those models into working applications."

Cathy O'Neil and Rachel Schutt include an important addendum in their definition, "A data scientist is someone who knows how to extract meaning from and interpret data, which requires both tools and methods from statistics and machine learning, as well as being human."

The growth of interest in data science is due to the rise of big data and the search for ways of managing and making sense of it. The term big data has been around for a while, but it typically refers to the digital trail that people generate when online, as well as machine-generated data that is shared by smart devices at home and at work.

According to Bernard Marr, "The term Big Data refers to the collection of all this data and our ability to use it to our advantage across a wide range of areas, including business."

Big data gets its name from its volume (the size of data generated), velocity (the speed of data generation), variety (of different types of data involved) and veracity (the trustworthiness of the data).

The first challenge with big data is simply cleaning and managing it. This can begin with data munging, which means transforming data points into something useable. Data engineers are then required to make the data workable for storage and processing.

These data-managing challenges are less of a problem with organisational data than with big data scraped from the web. The challenge with organisational data (in other words, data which comes from internal social media, surveys, HR information systems, enterprise management systems, and so on) is to really understand what the data points are and what comprises them. There are very few human capital standards and common definitions to rely on.

Even in the realm of human capital measurement, where companies have had a focus for many years, understanding the data that is collected and tracked is difficult.

You only need to think of terms like high potential, high performer and regretted turnover to realise the problems in defining those terms consistently and in a way that takes account of individual performance and impact.

This is one reason why organisational data is much harder to work with than a lot of the data which are pulled from the web and that often make up big data sets.

The second challenge with big data is how to make sense of it. There are issues with applying classical statistical techniques to big data, so analytics often depend on using inductive, pattern-recognition algorithms to search for findings instead.

These can be automated through machine learning approaches. Many of the common algorithms that are used for this are not new. They have been around for a long time. But because of the volume and velocity of big data they can now be now run at speed, taking advantage of modern computing power.

In classical statistics, hypotheses are developed from theory and tested and explored in controlled samples to understand and isolate key factors. This is sometimes referred to as frequentist statistics and it relies on things like confidence intervals. In working with big data, it's more the case of bashing through lots of different analyses to see what comes out the other end.

As such, data science is less about hypothesis-based reasoning and more like inductive (pattern-based) reasoning instead. This is an important change. It is more of a bottom-up approach. Patterns are determined by experimentation and iteration. It's common to use Bayesian inference and to look at probability and likelihood. These are calculation-intensive approaches, which depend on the huge gains that have been made in processing power.

Integrated analytics and GDPR

The application of these approaches in the employee engagement field is already beginning to have a significant impact.

Firstly, data science provides a great opportunity for more integrated analysis. Companies are able to connect their data in new and exciting ways. At a simple level, this means you can report customer and operational outcomes in the same tools as engagement findings. It also means you can track how employee interactions with customers align with feedback from customers. You can examine how actual patterns of interaction, for example through emails and instant messages, match up to perceptions of collaboration and potential roadblocks. It's possible to look at the impact of particular training programmes on the effectiveness of specific managers' teams, and so on.

Integrated analytics is a huge opportunity, and as the next chapter shows, it's the central focus of the shift to employee experience. However, there is one serious caveat to companies' attempts at data integration, which is data privacy.

The General Data Protection Regulation (GDPR) of the EU came into force in May 2018 and gives individuals control over their personal data. The regulation means that business processes that handle personal data must be designed and built with key safeguards to protect data. This might include, for example, using pseudonymization or full anonymization where appropriate. GDPR also means using the highest-possible privacy settings by default.

One key result of GDPR is that most companies are treading very lightly when it comes to integrating the data they hold on their employees with other data sets they may also have access to.

Given that data science relies on mashing together large and complicated data sets and examining the patterns that arise, there is a natural tension with GDPR, which effectively says keep hold of only what you absolutely need and in the most restricted way possible.

Informed consent is also at the heart of GDPR, which means you need very high trust in the workforce in order to proceed with integrated analytics.

As Bernard Marr points out, "Consent is a critical pillar of the legislation, and GDPR states that companies can only use personal data for the express purpose for which it was given. For HR teams, this means employees must explicitly opt in to allow their employer to use their personal data, and they must be made fully aware of how that data will be used."

The second data science opportunity for the employee engagement field is automated analysis.

One area where this has become commonplace is in human capital reporting, which has been largely automated through HR and human capital reporting systems.

Originally, these gave business leaders and HR partners dashboards of key people metrics. They now also use predictive analytics that are automated in the background to highlight key people risks, such as high turnover and potential talent shortages.

In the future, there will continue to be more automated analysis of people data, which will include tracking the experience of individuals and cohorts through the employee life cycle.

The third key opportunity is continuous listening via social media. This includes bot-driven surveys on social platforms, which are discussed in more depth in the next chapters.

The social platforms themselves provide automated tracking of engagement and sentiment, just as on external social media, and this is the area where big data science will have the biggest transformative effective on internal communications and engagement analytics.

The challenge for organisations will be to turn this listening activity away from tracking and surveillance and towards conversation and constructive dialogue, in order to build trust and to drive meaningful change.

A qualitative revolution

A massive pool of data is non-numeric and unstructured, in other words text, images, sound and video. As a result there has been an explosion of interest in using qualitative data more effectively in employee research. Being able to use machine learning and data science to make sense of this human and messy data is a huge opportunity.

Of course, qualitative data analysis has been around for a long time, originating in fields like anthropology and ethnography. This work is often intensive, requiring time and resources for data capture and processing. Fieldwork includes interviews, focus groups, observation, conversation and discourse analysis, and so on.

Analytics are derived by review and reflection, coding, and deconstructing narrative and symbols. It is a largely iterative process of categorising data into concepts, connecting those concepts, and then looking for corroborative evidence.

Some academics have referred to a modern qualitative revolution in organisational research, which mirrors the quantitative revolution in social science in the 1960s and 1970s. In particular, qualitative research provides more critical insights into root causes and the opportunity for more reflexivity, in other words checking how assumptions prompt a particular understanding of what's going on.

In the employee survey world, qualitative data has largely been restricted to feedback collected through open questions that are often asked at the end of a questionnaire. A typical question is something like, "What one change would most improve the company as a place to work?"

Answers are often categorised by themes and key words. Sometimes respondents categorise their own answers by selecting from a list of themes. Software was also developed which used large and detailed lexicons of terms, sometimes in many languages. These could be used for detailed reporting and basic sentiment analysis.

In all this, it's clear that qualitative researchers were really the poor cousins of the number crunchers in the employee survey firms. For a long time, there was a largely token effort at collecting open feedback. Why? Well, in paper surveys, it is expensive to transcribe written comments. When you are dealing with multi-language surveys, translation becomes a problem. The volume of comments make them difficult to analyse at a company-overall level. Sometimes employees might write things they could later regret. All in all, comments were difficult to deal with for a long period of time.

The opportunity to do more with survey comments and with qualitative data more broadly, given organisations are awash with it, is hugely exciting.

The data science approach for dealing with text is Natural Language Processing (NLP). This is a sub-field of artificial intelligence that is focused on enabling computers to understand and process human language. It originated with fairly simple language models and has developed into convolutional neural networks and deep learning.

The application of NLP has led to things like translation software, understanding of semantics and the summarisation of text. These machine analytics reduce the need for manual effort, but they work best at scale, as do most big data solutions.

The application of these approaches is revolutionising the field of employee insights. Employee surveys can be shorter in length because they now include more open questions that provide richer feedback that can be coded, analysed and reported using NLP tools.

There are also improved ways of visualisation comments data, through things like concept clouds and heat maps. Alongside these improvements, hot topics can be summarised in natural language and assessed in terms of sentiment. Analytics can also provide measures of popularity and consensus, plus detailed segmentation analysis.

Applications can now use machine intelligence to analyse chat-based conversations in real time. These virtual focus groups can include hundreds of people at once and feel more like a conversation than a survey. They can be used to investigate topics in more detail or to generate ideas.

Increasingly, these chat-based tools are running automatically in the background as bots. They are embedded within internal social media platforms and team threads, and can collect feedback at times that reflect employees' own personal milestones.

Similar deep learning approaches can also be applied to the analytics of images, in order to classify them, and detect and recognise objects. These approaches are still in their infancy in employee research, but in consumer research they are taking off.

For example, IKEA analyses how its customers show off their products in their own homes on photos they post on Instagram and elsewhere. This helps them to refine the way they display those same products in its catalogue and on its website. They also analyse the pictures that customers post when they are in the store, in order to improve the shopping experience.

It is easy to speculate on how image content analysis can be applied to employees' posts on internal and external social media in order to understand the current mood of employees and how they are sharing news of your company and its products and services online.

Moving on from the employee engagement era

These developments are leading to a renewed focus in employee research, which has languished without much innovation for a period of time. Some of the problems caused by packaged engagement surveys and solutions are being reduced by the ability to explore new questions in new ways. There is a new energy and creativity in employee research.

New technologies are leading to greater agility and flexibility, as well as more immediacy. Now, as well as surveying people about their intentions, it's possible to corroborate those opinions against actual behaviours, which can be measured and analysed in real time.

It's one thing to understand employees' attitudes to collaboration, but that analysis is much more powerful when it's combined with actual patterns of email communication and meetings.

You can understand people's stated intention to stay or leave for another employer, but you get a better picture of what's going on when you also observe the trigger behaviours that occurred before people have actually left.

In essence, this is the transformation that is underway now as companies move from thinking about employee engagement in isolation towards building a more holistic view of employee experience.

In the next chapter, I will show how by embracing employee experience, employee research can recapture some of the vitality, rigour and fresh-thinking that was more present in the golden age of employee research than in the employee engagement era.

I will highlight how new tools and approaches mean employee research can move on from employee engagement.

7. Employee Experience (EX)

This book has charted the changing world of work and looked at how the employee insights industry has adapted.

The traditional employment deal is long gone. Instead, companies now have to manage a tension between pushing responsibility and risk onto individuals versus the need to build collective trust and loyalty. The trust gap that exists in many companies as a result is a drag on performance. This is especially true at a time when business growth depends more than ever on employees' own innovation, creativity and service.

Many organisations have tried to close the trust gap by instituting routines for capturing employee voice. You have to work hard to gauge employees' opinions in an effective way. Otherwise, many people simply default to silence.

Those routines have often been survey-based. Surveys began by measuring morale, then satisfaction and latterly engagement. Many companies have achieved a lot by focusing on employee engagement, but there are problems with standardised products, which can limit their effectiveness.

In an age of big data and social media, there are opportunities to do more integrated and continuous listening and to better understand the messy, complicated experience of working for a company.

That's the promise held out by the next chapter in the history of employee insights and which is often labelled as employee experience (EX).

From employee engagement to employee experience

A number of people and organisations have started to explore what employee experience is and how to use it. One of those is Jacob Morgan. In his book *The Employee Experience Advantage*, Jacob defines EX as "the intersection of employee expectations, needs, and wants and the organisational design of those expectations, needs, and wants."

Jacob is dismissive of traditional employee engagement programmes, which, in his words, have "become the new annual review." At best, he says, engagement in many organisations "acts as an adrenaline shot to temporarily boost employee happiness."

By contrast, employee experience is about "designing an organisation where people want to show up by focusing on the cultural, technological, and physical environments."

It's a long-term process based on human-centred design. The best companies use analytics to really understand their workforce and they "have mastered the art and science of creating employee experiences."

Tracy Maylett and Matthew Wride in their book *The Employee Experience*, define EX as "creating an operating environment that inspires your people to do great things." As such, it is "the sum of perceptions employees have about their interactions with the organisation in which they work."

One of the key problems Tracy and Matthew identify in many organisations is the existence of expectation gaps. These occur when there is a mismatch between what people have been promised and what they believe they've been promised.

"Gaining alignment and understanding, and managing the Expectation Gap, is all about developing mutual respect, trust, and understanding in your organisation, because that's what leads to real, deep engagement."

An organisation's promises are tested during key moments ("moments of truth"). These moments can include regular events such as an induction or a promotion, or a life-stage event such as a period of leave, or a business event such as a restructuring. They are points when trust is either built or diminished, depending on the nature of the experience that is delivered and received.

What both books highlight is that EX is a big idea. EX relates to the individual and their entire relationship with their employer. It's a reflection of things like culture and purpose, as well as the day-to-day and practical.

It's not the same as user experience – which is about how easy a particular tool, piece of software or process is. And it's not to be confused with HR customer experience – your satisfaction when interacting with the function. EX may be the culmination of smaller moments, and some of those key moments fall under HR's domain, but in its entirety EX is very large in scope. It is all-encompassing.

EX is a bottom-up view of the organisation

To my mind, employee experience can be thought of as simply "What's it like to work here?" From the run up to your first day, to the end of your first month, to your first anniversary, to a promotion, and so on, until you leave. Perhaps you're a freelancer just doing a short piece of work for a company. Maybe you're on a secondment or you're an intern. The same question remains when it comes to EX: What's it like to work here?

Is it a place where you can be yourself or do you have to put on a game face and try to fit in? Are people friendly? Do they collaborate well? If you do a good job, do people recognise it? When you accomplish a big goal, do people celebrate it? Is it somewhere you can learn new things? Is it a place where you can make a positive impact, on customers, the community and the environment?

What's important about all these questions is that they begin with the employee. And by employee here, I am referring to anyone working for the company whether in a full-time role, a part-time position, a contractor or a free agent. EX is about capturing their perspective. It's a bottom-up, personalised and individual view of the organisation.

Employee engagement, on the other hand, is fundamentally a management question. It's a top-down perspective. It's the view from managers in an organisation looking at their workforce.

Employee engagement is about making sure people are connected to the goals and purpose of the company. Are people enabled to do their job well without red-tape getting in the way or poor technology holding them back? Do people feel energised to go the extra mile in their job when it comes to dealing with customer questions? Do people buy into the company's strategy and understand its direction?

Employee engagement measurement, therefore, is like an audit. It's about ensuring processes, programmes and people are aligned and working effectively.

In fact, many organisations adopt this kind of process view when it comes to their engagement programmes. Engagement is often part of an overall quality management framework. Engagement scores are included in the annual report alongside other key performance indicators like profit, turnover and cash flow.

Employee experience is a conversation

Employee experience is more like a conversation. What's on your mind? How are you finding things? Are they what you expected? The output is less structured and feedback needs to be captured in the moment. It's a more human view of culture and work challenges.

This shift in perspective from employee engagement to EX is one that many organisations are thinking about. This is in response to the changes that are happening in their workforce and in the economy, that we have already described, which require greater trust and openness.

A focus on individual experiences also reflects a shift in behavioural science to understand how individuals can be nudged to change their behaviour through personalised cues and messages. EX measurement is also only possible because of new tools and technologies, especially the increased use of social media.

In this chapter and the next, I will show how companies are adapting to EX. It's not an easy transformation. It poses a challenge because of the change in perspective that's needed.

It's often a case of turning things on their head. It requires putting the employee at the heart of your thinking.

Engagement fits easily into a traditional management mindset. It's one of its advantages. With engagement, leaders are directing employees and managing their effectiveness.

With EX the picture is more personal and conversational, and it's driven by employees themselves, often in a messy and complicated fashion. As a result, it can be harder to manage by traditional means.

EX requires a leadership mindset that is more about enabling individuals and teams rather than directing tasks and managing resources.

EX leadership requires empathy and design thinking, as well as the ability to provide support and to give inspiration across shifting and diverse networks.

This EX leadership challenge is the focus of the final chapter of this book.

Before then, let's first look at two companies that are already putting EX into practice.

EX in practice at Arm

Arm is often described as Britain's most successful technology company. It is the world's leading provider of silicon intellectual property and custom system-on-a-chips. Its designs are at the heart of billions of devices, including smartphones and anything connected to the Internet of Things. In 2016, Arm was acquired by SoftBank Group's Vision Fund.

Arm is a company that depends on the human ingenuity of its staff. It is fab-less, in other words the company doesn't manufacture anything. Rather, it licenses its intellectual property and designs across an ecosystem of partners and customers.

A high proportion of its staff are software engineers and have PhDs. The company is headquartered in Cambridge, in the heart of the UK's Silicon Fen. It also has staff in San Jose, Bangalore and other small offices around the world.

I have worked with Arm since 2014, when Simon Segars took over as CEO. At that point, the company had experienced extremely rapid growth. Employee numbers had increased from 1,700 to 3,900 people in a short period of 5 years.

As the company became larger and more corporate, leaders were concerned about not becoming bureaucratic. They wanted to continue to work in ways that were simple and fast. They also needed to update their physical work space. In 2014, I remember that white boards were a common sight in corridors, which functioned as makeshift meeting spaces.

The focus of their employee survey was on understanding Arm's cultural "secret sauce", so they could preserve and sustain the critical elements as the company continued to grow in the future. Arm's HR strategy was focused on three key planks: talent, leadership and culture.

Sasha Watson is VP of Employee Experience at Arm. Her role covers the end-to-end employee experience in EMEA, the USA and APAC, from pre-hire to retire. Her remit spans shared services, recruitment, learning and development, internal communications, research and people analytics, internal events, diversity and inclusion, facilities, volunteering and community relations.

As you can tell, the focus of EX at Arm is broad. Above all, it is about improving organisational effectiveness. EX is about working on culture, leadership and structure.

There are two layers to thinking about employee experience at Arm.

The first is Brilliant Basics. This means getting the foundations right, like systems that are easy to use, having a great line manager, and being able to plan a fulfilling career.

The second is Moments that Matter. These are the key moments that are pivotal to employees' time at Arm.

The moments that matter were identified by analysing the results to the engagement surveys for key cohorts, and by looking at the recurring themes that came up in town hall meetings and during site visits.

The HR team distilled an initial list of 15 moments down to five pivotal ones. These include on-boarding (especially day one) and off-boarding (the process of leaving). They include moments when

121

an employee's pace of contributing may be affected by a family need or a well-being challenge. The fifth pivotal moment is when someone becomes a senior leader. This is a key moment for the individual, of course, but it's also important because of the impact that person will have on the rest of the Arm community.

According to Sasha, "At Arm, employee experience is about moments and events that leave a positive impression, but it is mainly about achieving our vision of ensuring people thrive every day in a place they love to work." The EX role ensures connectivity. By thinking end-to-end, it removes frustrations – in Sasha's words, by "invisibly enabling people."

It's also critical to make sure there's a balance between building a global framework and allowing for local execution. "We don't want to do the same thing everywhere. There has to be local ownership. The impact should feel the same, in terms of values and community, but your Day One will be celebrated differently in Bangalore (with much more razzmatazz) than in San Jose. However, the feeling you have, that you are able to thrive at Arm, needs to be the same."

Everything is experience at Landsec

At Landsec, everything is about experience. In fact, this is its core brand philosophy with respect to customers, communities, partners and employees. Landsec is one of the largest commercial property development and Real Estate Investment Trusts in the UK. The company owns and manages offices, shopping and leisure destinations in London and elsewhere in the UK. Its buildings include the iconic Piccadilly Lights, the Nova building near Victoria and Bluewater shopping centre in Kent.

Landsec is at the leading edge of changes in the workplace, as their tenants' expectations regarding flexibility, technology and the work environment are changing rapidly.

I started working with Landsec in 2011 as Rob Noel succeeded Francis Salway as CEO. Rob inherited a fairly traditional, establishment-type organisation. He was very involved in designing and championing its first companywide employee survey. That survey gave him a base line as he sought to build a more performance-oriented culture. In his words, "a culture with more of an edge."

Over successive years, engagement consistently improved at Landsec, as the company embarked on a series of transformations, using insights from employee surveys to drive positive change.

One of the key areas it has focused on is performance management. The Landsec HR team looked in depth at the way performance management worked across the business. It's one of the key processes that impacts employee experience broadly. They moved to a new platform to help simplify the process, but the real change was improving the quality of conversation.

They looked at the frequency and the content of performance-related discussions in order to understand how to improve two-way feedback. They calculated that around 70 per cent of employee relations issues could likely have been stopped if there had been an earlier, more effective conversation.

They also sought to drive a greater alignment between employee experience and customer experience. Rather than each employee having as many as 8-10 objectives, which were based on key performance indicators, they moved to using only a few "impact statements". Those statements relate to how employees can improve the experience of their direct customer, whether that is another team or department, a partner, or a customer of the company.

In 2017, Landsec accelerated its transformation towards a more customer-led culture by moving to a new head office, in one of their own key developments in Victoria in London.

This move wasn't approached as simply a change of surroundings. The goal was to transform the way people work and to establish a new approach to employee experience. According to Sue Greenland, Head of HR, London at Landsec, "We knew we wanted our employees to feel autonomous, trusted and heard. We wanted to build a company that was inclusive, collaborative and future-proof."

"We implemented activity-based working (not hot-desking) by providing multiple spaces for our teams and partners to work in, we adopted activity-based dressing by encouraging our people to "dress for your day", and we enabled flexible working by providing mobile technology and tools to manage teams from afar." These were big and highly-visible changes for what remained a quite traditional organisation.

According to Sue, "We wanted to align the office environment with the kind of culture we want to create. We tested a lot of the important ideas before we moved, trialling new work spaces and new technology with some teams while we were still in our old offices."

A key goal for the new work space was to improve well-being and social collaboration. The office includes a juice bar and free healthy snacks in a social hub. They set up white-noise machines at strategic points in open-plan areas to reduce background distractions and increase privacy levels without the need for physical walls. The building maximises access to natural light and, important for a central London location, it was set up for better air quality and sustainability.

Over 90 per cent of employees thought the new work space improved the work culture. There was a subsequent reduction of almost 20 per cent in internal emails, as people were more able to speak face-to-face. Printing reduced by almost two-thirds as people now used tablets and social hubs to share and view information.

At the end of 2017, the whole company attended a two-day workshop in order to come up with new ways to create fantastic experiences for customers. "This was an immersive training programme for all employees designed to enhance our customer-led culture. It was an important investment in our brand, ensuring that our 'Everything is Experience' philosophy is transformed into action across the business."

"The objective was to help employees understand what our new brand means in terms of how we can enhance experience for all our customers. Our definition of customers includes our occupiers but also their employees, shoppers, visitors, local communities, partners and our colleagues."

It was decided that the training would include all staff, from all sites and all levels, so employees got to spend time with people from other teams to help broaden their perspective on the business.

On top of this, each team was tasked with coming up with its own 90-day action plan for improving their own customers' experience.

The whole programme was championed by the top 25 senior leaders within the business, even though this was a significant investment in time and resources. It's an example of effective EX leadership, which is discussed in the final chapter, as it included a focus on learning, and especially building line of sight for employees in terms of their own contribution to the company's purpose and ambition.

Overall, the training was an exercise in CX-EX alignment. In the retail sector, for example, shopping destinations can achieve higher "dwell time" and average spend per visit by providing a great visitor experience based on a strong mix of retail, food and leisure. A growing number of online brands are also using physical stores to create compelling brand experiences. There was a need to bring that kind of outside thinking into Landsec, so that in return, "we can use our experience to provide customers with great experiences," said Sue.

In order to embed the culture change, EX measurement plays a key role. Not only through employee engagement surveys and pulse surveys, but also by integrating CX measurement. This includes getting feedback from internal (inter-departmental) customers as well as measuring external customer satisfaction.

According to Sue, "HR now uses EX as a key lens. We focus on values, behaviours and individual experiences. We still have a lot more to do as there are some areas where a "one size fits all" mentality still remains. But we are focusing much more on personalising choices for employees."

Performance marketing

These client stories show how some leading companies have already started to achieve a lot by focusing on EX. They are exploring new ways of capturing employee voice, shaping a compelling work environment and building high levels of trust. But we are only in the first few years of this emerging science. To see how it will evolve into more common practice in the years ahead, we can look at the transition that has occurred in advertising and marketing, as well as in business intelligence. In all these areas there have been dramatic changes. It's the argument of this book that a similar transformation is happening in employee insights and HR.

Marketing, sales, advertising and customer relationship management have all been transformed by big data, which primarily come from digital platforms and social media.

As evidence of this, Accenture, whose main business is technology consulting and outsourcing, is now one of the largest advertising agencies in the world. Accenture Interactive (its digital business) is one of a number of Cagencies (consultancy-agencies) benefiting from large-scale opportunities at the intersection of technology, data and analytics.

This is because the traditional advertising agency has seen its world shaken up. Its competitors now include Amazon, Google and Facebook. Clients (advertisers) have responded to the new landscape by building in-house advertising teams who work directly with these digital platforms, cutting out the middleman. Advertisers are then looking for help from the likes of Accenture with analytics in order to optimise their advertising spend.

This is largely due to the rise of performance marketing, in other words when advertisers only pay once a specific action is completed, such as an impression, a click or a lead. To be successful, you need to target and personalise advertising messages as much as possible. This is where data and analytics can provide a competitive advantage.

Companies are using automated machine learning to do things like sentiment analysis, audience analysis and image analysis. They're using these tools to recognise patterns and to develop a better understanding of consumer behaviour.

Broadly, digital marketing analytics fall into three different categories. First, they are used to understand the relationship between different marketing channels. Second, they are a way to optimise the revenue attributed to specific marketing efforts and campaigns. Third, they are used to build a better picture of the buyer's journey. The final of these categories has led to a huge growth of interest in Customer Experience (CX).

Customer Experience (CX)

According to Alan Pennington, CX is a discipline which involves "understanding what matters to customers, actively designing critical experiences, equipping teams to deliver on that design and connecting the customer outcomes to the bottom line."

The challenge is to create "a consistently good experience that meets the expectation created by your brand and to know where it is possible to exceed those expectations at a critical moment. It is the cumulative impact of small changes that creates an improved experience and contributes to an evolution of the customer culture."

A key tool for CX is customer journey mapping. This is a structured way to understand and capture customers' wants, needs and expectations at each stage of their experience with your company. It is not the same as a process map, but rather a tool for visualising how customers interact with an organisation across multiple channels and touch points.

A journey map is composed of a customer life cycle, which is divided into stages. At each stage are a series of interactions (often called touch points) that the customer has with your business. Understanding which of these moments really matter and then tweaking the service experience is one way of optimising performance.

For Pennington, the aim is to build trust through these experiences and by the smart use of data and analytics. "As you look to design more personalised experiences, one of the key components that will enable you to do this is access to personal information on your customers."

The experience economy

The shift to CX is a recognition that the new battleground for many companies is in the realm of experience.

This change was first identified by Joseph Pine and James Gilmore in 1998 who described the emergence of the experience economy: "Goods and services are no longer enough to foster economic growth, create new jobs, and maintain economic prosperity. To realize revenue growth and increased employment, the staging of experiences must be pursued as a distinct form of economic output. Indeed, in a world saturated with largely undifferentiated goods and services the greatest opportunity for value creation resides in staging experiences."

Pine and Gilmore highlighted how successful companies stage engaging experiences through mass customisation: "Mass customising – efficiently serving customers uniquely – means producing only and exactly what individual customers want. Mass customising any good turns that good automatically into a service; and mass customising any service turns that service automatically into an experience."

One of the key points Pine and Gilmore make is that while services provide a value, experiences are memorable. This is really critical. In today's economy, organisations are in the memory business, creating moments that provide impact. The emotional chord that is established as a result is the key to customer retention, loyalty and sales growth. Hence, it's not enough to simply measure customer satisfaction, or customer sacrifice ("the gap between what a customer settles for and what they want exactly"). The best companies elevate measurement to capture "customer surprise" and even "customer suspense".

With the rise in e-commerce and digital business, companies have put an increasing focus on designing customer experiences and using customer insights effectively. This is not restricted to the design of the user experience (the ease of using a product) and the user interface (the ease of using a piece of software), but to the whole series of interactions that a customer has with your company across multiple moments and touch points. In other words, the total customer experience.

Customer-intelligent companies use insights from across all these moments to create memorable experiences through mass customisation. In fact, increasingly, experiences are being co-created with customers, so that rather than just "personalised customisation" we are moving towards an era of "collaborative customisation" (tailoring a service to meet a customer's unique requirements, based on a dialogue or a self-service approach).

In his 2015 book *"X"*, Brian Solis argues that experience is the single most important thing in any business, but is often neglected by executives: "In an always-on world where everyone is connected to information and also one another, experience is your brand."

For Solis, what's key is experience architecture. "The future of business is experiential, depending on creating and cultivating meaningful experiences."

Integrated business intelligence

The shift to digital marketing is a huge transformation for many businesses. It provides new opportunities for engaging with customers by creating compelling experiences and winning new business. As a result, the marketing function has gained a more strategic role in many organisations.

This has also happened alongside the development of Customer Relationship Management (CRM) software, which makes it easier to manage interactions with current and potential customers and to use data about those interactions to improve customer retention and to drive new sales.

The datafication of marketing and sales is allied to the rise of integrated business intelligence more generally. This is possible because most large companies use an Enterprise Resource Planning platform to integrate the management of core business processes, including accounting, procurement, sales and operations. Enterprise planning software has grown rapidly into a huge industry. Companies are looking to maximise the effectiveness of that investment by using analytics to optimise performance across their core processes.

It is important to incorporate an analysis of customer experiences within that data architecture, which is one reason why some enterprise systems include customer feedback platforms. In this way, early customer signals from operational data can be combined with customer insights for an integrated approach to improving CX performance.

Many organisations have also built a centralised business intelligence team whose job it is to integrate data across all aspects of performance, in order to provide updates to leaders, to look for connections and to visualise data patterns, and to drive greater efficiency and effectiveness.

People analytics

In all these developments, however, it can feel like the employee side of things is being left behind. Sales, marketing, technology, operations and finance are all involved in centralised business intelligence, but where is HR?

The related employee intelligence field in the HR function is often called people analytics (or sometimes HR analytics or workforce analytics).

Interest in people analytics has certainly grown over time. Only ten years ago it was rare to come across much analytical work in HR beyond human capital reporting, compensation and workforce planning. Now, according to Deloitte's Human Capital Trends Report, 77 per cent of companies believe people analytics is important.

Deloitte defines people analytics as "the use of people-related data to improve and inform all types of management, business, and HR decisions throughout the company."

They claim that "the people analytics revolution is gaining speed. While HR organisations have been talking about building analytics teams for several years, we see a major leap forward in capabilities."

However, despite this apparent growth of interest, progress in analytics in HR is lagging behind that of other functions.

For example, a report by the New Talent Management Network (NTMN) concluded that "only basic people analytics are being performed by most organisations."

Janet Marler and John Boudreau conducted an evidence-based review of HR analytics and also concluded that "despite evidence linking the adoption of HR analytics to organisational performance, the adoption of HR analytics is very low."

A study by Alec Levenson and Gillian Pillans for the Corporate Research Forum concluded that, "Our research indicates a sizeable gap between the rhetoric and the reality of workforce analytics. For most HR functions, this is an emerging field. We found only 7 per cent of organisations have reached a reasonably advanced level. Organisations have a great deal to do before they are able to routinely deploy workforce analytics to improve business outcomes."

One reason for this lack of impact is that many HR people do not have the analytical skills needed. Traditionally, HR has focused more on legal and compliance matters or on skills like facilitation and negotiation.

Another reason is that employee data is fundamentally different and harder to work with than customer data. Customers often only have a transactional relationship with a vendor. It is usually short-term, one-off or periodic. This makes it relatively simple to consider experiences and outcomes.

By contrast, an employment relationship is longer-term, more continuous and far deeper. Motivation and experience at work are complicated relationships, which bring into play one's own personality and characteristics, financial and personal circumstances, as well as values, identity, meaning, purpose and trust.

There is also the problem that employee insights are often most useful when they're anonymous. As Josh Bersin points out, "While ratings in a consumer setting may or may not be anonymous, at work anonymity is critical. In the consumer world, if you poorly review a restaurant or 'down rate' a driver, there are likely no major consequences to you – in fact it can be a good thing, because the company can get back to you to address your problem. At work, the ramifications are different. If you 'down rate' your boss or say something critical about him (even in a constructive way), you may be labelled a 'trouble maker', which now reflects poorly on you."

So although companies have been keen to find a competitive advantage in the analysis of their market, customer and operational data, they haven't made the same progress with their people data.

In fact, it's more common to place a premium on playing things safe by keeping HR data simple and high level. When it comes to people analytics there is often a focus on risk management and compliance, rather than on identifying opportunities to improve business performance and productivity.

The main focus for most people analytics teams at the present time is workforce planning and reporting. In large organisations, this is being automated by technologies whose analytical capabilities are increasingly impressive. They are able to provide leaders across an organisation with real-time updates on key measures like turnover, recruitment and utilisation.

In smaller organisations that cannot afford these smart systems, the whole area of human capital reporting can remain a problem. Many smaller companies still rely on Excel and have problems with basic data quality.

This problem with HR data quality was recently highlighted by work which looked at the accuracy of gender pay gap reporting in the UK. Around 15 per cent of submissions contained errors. Nigel Marriot of the Royal Statistical Society who led the research concluded that, "People working in HR are largely left on their own to figure out the calculations, even though many of these staff will never have had statistics training."

To really embrace the potential of employee experience, and to understand employee attitudes and behaviour through the lens of EX, requires a new science and tool kit. In fact, EX provides a whole new domain for people analytics (and for business intelligence inside most organisations).

The biggest opportunity is to do more with the individual-level data that are being captured more frequently and continuously inside organisations. The biggest challenge is to do this in ways which build trust, rather than potentially damaging trust further. In order to achieve this, many companies are starting small and they are using employee journey maps as their organising framework. They are also focusing on specific key talent groups.

EX journey maps

A focus on employee journeys is really at the heart of any kind of EX activity. That's because it provides a way of organising information from the perspective of the employee – how they view

132

the organisation and what's happening at any point. A journey map helps connect individual points of view to broader organisational outcomes.

According to Alan Pennington, the aim of an employee journey map is to provide "a common framework and language to engage with the employee experience."

It can help you to improve engagement. It can help you identify quick wins, as well as more strategic change opportunities. A journey map can contribute to an overall culture change, especially in the case of digital transformation. It can help by bringing employee voice to the decision making process. It can also connect employees to the external customer journey.

An EX journey map often follows the employee life cycle. The life cycle provides the back bone. At a high level, this can be as simple as how you hire people, build their capability, engage people, retain people and lead people. It can also include the exit process (and perhaps the alumni network that you may want to create).

Under each of these key stages, you can build a micro-map, which has more specific and detailed employee journeys around key moments or touch points. In addition, you can tailor those micro-maps for different segments and cohorts.

Moments that matter

What are those key moments? They include formal moments such as performance reviews, informal touch points such as team meetings, and other factors such as the physical work space and technology. They can also be business events like product launches or organisational changes and restructuring.

The moments that matter the most are best identified through evidence and conversation. The ones to focus on are those that are both important and painful. One measure of importance, for example, is the impact they have on engagement. Pain means they create problems if they're not working well, in terms of dissatisfaction or wasted effort or poor collaboration, quality, service or safety.

Most organisations will focus at a high level on the key moments that affect all employees and then build micro-maps for looking at the most important touch points in more detail. They will also review those micro-maps for the specific, key talent groups that are identified from their people strategy.

For example, many of my clients have identified digital talent as a key group for achieving their business transformation successfully. A key challenge is how to attract, engage and retain those employees with a background in, for example, coding and digital tools. They may have a very different set of expectations, needs and wants from your majority employee base.

Consider, for example, that you are an investment bank or a law firm watching the rise of new competitors in the fields of fin-tech and law-tech. You face the daunting task of attracting and then successfully integrating non-traditional employees with key technology skills. In order to be successful, you need to be able to tailor and articulate your value proposition (which is the promise you make about the employee experience) and ensure you deliver on that promise across all the key moments.

One of the key moments that matter for groups like these is performance management. Digital work teams that are agile, global and virtual require a frequent cadence of feedback, a culture of openness and transparency, and there's a need to recognise team performance and collaboration over and above individual contribution.

This can provide a challenge for traditional performance management systems, which focus on individual goals and objectives. It is one reason why many companies are recognising the need to modernise their approach to performance management by placing more emphasis on continuous feedback and by de-emphasising individual ratings and performance scores. (This is what Landsec did, as described earlier in this chapter.)

Critical talent cohorts

Another key talent group that companies often focus on is graduates. This can be a group that is expensive to recruit and train.

Some companies also face a problem that at the end of a graduate programme, when having trained a class of future leaders, those graduates are then tempted away by a competitor who benefits from the investment you have made.

There is often an ongoing debate in large companies on the pros and cons of graduate recruits. They are seen as a visible commitment to the future, but also a pain to manage effectively. The question of return on investment hangs like a grey cloud over everyone's heads.

An EX lens on your graduate programme can help improve outcomes. You can collect feedback through all stages, from the application and assessment process through to on-boarding, the first-day, the end of the first week, and so on.

One useful feature of a graduate programme, from an analytical point of view, is that graduates normally enrol as a class. This means you can track individuals in a class over time and also compare their experiences to other classes in previous years. You can review the differences in the experiences of individuals in a class who left, stayed or went on to be successful performers. You can analyse the moments when engagement was boosted or dissatisfaction arose. You can even test different experiences at those moments to see how this improves outcomes.

For example, often a key moment for a group like this is at the end of a rotation. How is feedback shared? How are learnings captured? What is the nature of the conversation about next steps and future options? How is the transition from one part of your graduate programme to another managed? All these questions are critical to achieving an effective experience.

Similar approaches can be taken for other talent groups such as expats, high potentials, experienced professionals, and so on.

The best companies don't just focus on the obvious groups. They do the work required to identify mission-critical talent groups. They do this by connecting workforce planning to their business goals through their people strategy.

The connection here is often the variability of performance. Where do you have roles, and people with key skills required for the future, that you see significant performance variability in things like productivity, sales and quality? These are roles which are often mission critical and where effective people management can make a huge difference. You will want to focus your EX efforts on these groups, in order to ensure high engagement at the key moments that matter.

The journey map provides a framework for organising EX analytics at the individual level and over time and in alignment with your business strategy. EX analytics is about identifying longitudinal patterns between critical talent cohorts.

This provides the best definition of EX from my point of view. Employee experience is about analysing individual journeys together and dynamically, so you can understand and improve events, touch points and processes in order to gain a systemic lift in productivity and performance.

Employee personas

A useful tool for making sense of EX data in this way is employee personas. This is another technique that comes straight from marketing.

In marketing, personas are a way of better understanding audiences, influencers and buyers. They are used to understand buying decisions and the people who make them. They can include a mix of demographic, behavioural and psychographic data (in other words, things like personality, values, opinions, attitudes, interests and lifestyles).

Adele Revella defines personas as, "An archetype; a composite picture of the real people who buy, or might buy, products like the ones you market, based on what you've learned in direct interviews with real buyers."

For Adele, a key component of building personas is qualitative, especially active listening through interviews and conversation. "If your personas are based on generic or internal ideas, your content won't be any better than it was before you had personas."

This is a bit different from how personas are used in product development. Personas of this type are created to represent the major needs and expectations of the different types of users of a website, product or service. They are often quite factual and needs based.

They are a way of improving the user experience of those specific tools.

It's also different from how personas are used in driving social media advocacy. This is done by reviewing online profiles, in order to identify different groups of influencers. These are based on the size of their networks and the role they play in amplifying your brand. The key components here are largely quantitative.

Marketing personas are far deeper in scope. "A marketing persona is a composite sketch of a key segment of your audience. For content marketing purposes, you need personas to help you deliver content that will be most relevant and useful to your audience."

The same thing applies to employee personas in an EX world. They provide a means for moving beyond traditional ways of segmenting your workforce, such as generations. They provide a far richer and more colourful mix of demographic, performance and attitudinal variables. They are a way of better understanding employee experiences, based on aggregating individual employee journeys.

To develop personas you need to look very broadly for sources of information. This can include surveys, focus groups, interviews and data from social media.

Each persona should include a set of top priorities. You should uncover how people view success. You should also include a list of potential frustrations and perceived barriers.

Personas help by providing a visual way of viewing EX data. They are normally written in the first person ("this is a priority for me"). This helps to reframe EX as an individual view of the organisation, in contrast to the top-down view of employee engagement that is more familiar to many leaders.

The best personas are focused on those critical talent groups for whom you are building detailed micro-maps of the employee journey. In this way, you can really zoom in to understand the moments that matter in great depth.

Employee experience is like a movie

Personas can help leaders to think differently about the workforce. For organisations to attract, retain and engage critical talent, they need to shift from focusing on the traditional elements of the employment deal to a more holistic view of experience. This includes understanding employee journeys and optimising the moments that matter. Just as for customer experience, this involves a shift in thinking. To quote Pine and Gilmore again: "Staging compelling experiences begins with embracing an experience-directed mindset."

In *The Experience Economy*, Pine and Gilmore argue that "all work is theatre". As such, strategy provides the drama, business processes are the script, the work itself is the theatre, and the offering is the performance.

Performers (employees) are at their best when they are inspired to follow the principles of great acting, such as being "in the present" (engaged). Leaders are most effective when they behave like great directors, focusing on casting, working collaboratively, staying in the moment, and managing the tension between learning and creativity.

The directing role requires organisational skills, interpretative skills and story-telling skills. During a performance, of course, the director is off-stage rather than the centre of attention, which is an important leadership lesson.

I would argue that employee experience is more like a movie (or a TV series or perhaps even a soap opera) than a play. This is because the end product comes from piecing together different scenes, episodes or moments into a consistent whole. The scenes occur at different times, in different places and with different people.

From an employee experience perspective, this means understanding all the interactions employees have with the organisation, from before they join, through the hiring process and on-boarding, through all the moments that matter as an employee, and potentially on to those involved with leaving the company and even re-joining in the future.

The leader/director's skill lies in aligning all the episodes delivered by multiple performers over time. A key success factor is collaboration. Movie production rarely begins with a finalised script. Instead, the script is adjusted and revised collaboratively with performers. And, as you see in the credits, a host of supporting roles have an impact on the final experience, from script writers to editors, CGI artists, technicians, costume designers, and so on.

Employee experience management is similarly a process of collaboration between HR, IT, business analytics, marketing, leadership and front-line managers. It is a joined-up approach to organisational design and capabilities, jobs, teams, rewards and the way people work. It encompasses individual and team effectiveness, as well as the physical workspace and the digital tools that employees use.

Thinking about employee experience management as movie-making, then talent management is casting, ensuring you have the right people lined up for your key roles. Employee journey maps are story boards, helping you optimise the key moments that matter. A persona is a character analysis, allowing leaders to better understand key talent segments. Learning and development is the discipline and craft of rehearsing. Collaboration is editing and personalising key moments. Leadership is directing – creating the conditions for people to perform at their best.

Pine and Gilmore wrote *The Experience Economy* in 1999. Today, increasingly, experiences are being co-created with customers and employees. The results are online, across social media, and they are transparent and public. One way to understand this is to look at your LinkedIn feed. If it's like mine, it includes people editing their own movies as their jobs and careers evolve.

For example, my feed includes people sharing pictures of their first day at work, showing their work space, equipment, new colleagues and welcome pack. It also includes people sharing news of a promotion or explaining the new role they're taking on and why they're excited about it. And it also includes farewells, often an image of a well-worn security pass and a commitment to stay in touch and to advocate for that company in the future.

In this sense, employee experience management is about creating the framework for people to produce and edit their own compelling movies online. If you're successful, then those stories will help to attract other talented people and reinforce the company's culture, in turn driving more collaboration, commitment and advocacy.

Design thinking

Even though employee experience is inherently messy and conversational, one key attribute of organisations that are good at EX is a design-thinking mindset.

Design-thinking is a bit of a buzzword and not everyone likes the way it is now applied outside of its original setting, which is product development and innovation. But it is a useful way of describing the change in perspective that is required in HR, from its traditional focus on compliance, process and policies to the design of moments, events and programmes that can lead to a systemic lift in engagement, collaboration and productivity.

Design thinking is a method used in developing products and services. It is human-centred and iterative. It really emerged with user experience design in software engineering. In fact, the computer scientist Herbert Simon was the first to mention design as a way of thinking in his 1969 book, *Sciences of the Artificial*. From the 1970s, design thinking continued to evolve before entering the mainstream in the 2000s.

Tim Brown is the CEO of the design agency IDEO, whose founder David Kelley was one of the first people to popularise the term outside of the design community. Tim is one of the foremost proponents of design thinking as a business process. In his 2009 book, *Change by Design*, he busts the myth of the lone-genius innovator. He argues instead that innovation comes from a team-based process of rigorous examination, through which great ideas are identified and developed before being realised as new offerings and capabilities.

It's common to think of that process as consisting of five steps: empathise, define, ideate, prototype, and test.

Design thinking begins with gaining an empathetic understanding of the problem you're trying to solve. This normally requires some form of user research, often interviews and observation. Empathy is crucial because it allows you to set aside your own assumptions in order to gain insight into users and their needs. They key question at this stage is not what the problem is, but why there is a problem.

During the define stage, it's important to analyse the information you have collected and to synthesise the findings in order to define the core problem you are looking to solve. This requires determining a clear and actionable problem statement.

The third stage is about generating ideas. With the knowledge you have gathered, you can start to identify new solutions to the problem statement you've created. You can look for alternative ways of viewing the problem. Often this phase involves brainstorming and then refining a list of ideas.

The prototype phase is about producing inexpensive, scaled-down versions of the product or service. In this way, you can investigate different solutions and gauge their impact on behaviours and outcomes. A common phrase applied to this stage is "fail early, fail often" (which has become a mantra in some sections of the tech industry).

In the final phase, you test the completed product using the best solutions identified during the prototype phase. Usually, this is an iterative process. In other words, results generated during the testing phase are used to further refine and solve the problems you are looking to fix.

For Tim Brown, what's most critical in this process is that design starts by understanding human behaviours, expectations, wants and needs. The best way of learning is to make prototypes. By trying things out, you can test and explore how they are used in practice and quickly discover what works and what doesn't. Design thinking also requires involving people by gaining their active participation and co-creation. In his words, "design is too important to be left to designers."

Design-thinking challenges for HR

All these steps pose a challenge for traditional HR thinking. In most companies, people policies are determined by small groups of specialists. Information is restricted on a need-to-know basis. Communications are closely managed. Decisions are based on compliance and risk management frameworks. Budgets and systems determine outcomes.

In HR, there is often a bias against prototyping because it's seen as safer to rely on things that are already used and accepted. There is also a reluctance to do much split testing in case it's viewed as being unfair by one or other of the groups. Testing also requires a degree of transparency that is often missing in typical HR communications.

These are all important reasons why traditional performance reviews continue to be common practice in most large organisations. Despite evidence that highlights the lack of effectiveness of traditional performance reviews and the high cost of running them, there is huge organisational inertia. They work to an extent. The potential risk of making a change is too great, so many companies simply stick to what they have.

This is why, in many cases, the shift to design-thinking requires an overhaul for traditional HR functions. It is one of the hardest elements of introducing a genuine EX approach in many companies.

Another challenge for HR is that design thinking's methods borrow from a variety of disciplines, including ethnography, computer science, psychology and behavioural science. Employees in HR tend to have a narrow range of skills and experience, for example in the areas of rewards, benefits or labour relations. Tim Brown argues that effective design thinkers are "T-shaped". In other words, they have a depth of expertise in order to make a tangible contribution, but also the capacity to work across disciplines in effective multidisciplinary teams.

In order to introduce EX into the function, many large companies have begun to establish the role of VP of Employee Experience (as at Arm). This role is often a "connector" – someone who is responsible for ensuring consistency across all the various HR teams and processes. They are often an experienced practitioner – someone who has worked as a business partner and in centres of expertise in corporate HR. In addition to connecting HR initiatives in new ways, they also need to connect HR to other business functions, especially marketing and business intelligence.

The EX maturity curve

In this emerging new science of EX, then, a number of key areas stand out. These include: a marketing mindset; integrated business analytics; using employee journeys as an organising framework; accessing a broader set of data; and adopting a design-thinking lens on programmes, workspaces and experiences.

In order to bring these different elements together, one idea that I've found useful, is assessing the maturity of an organisation in terms of its approach to EX. I typically think about this in two dimensions: insights and activation.

Insights here means using data to really understand employee journeys and experiences. Activation means the ability to apply that knowledge to improve processes, systems and programmes. It also means the ability to deliver meaningful change.

In the early stages of the maturity curve are organisations who are just starting to build EX capability and who probably collect insights through an annual engagement survey. Engagement survey results are likely to be looked at in isolation from other human capital data and even the results of other surveys. Key results from an engagement survey may be included in the company's annual report and some engagement insights may be included in recruitment materials. These can help with building a consistent approach to how the organisation markets itself to potential recruits on LinkedIn and elsewhere.

More mature organisations supplement their engagement survey with agile pulse surveys. This means they can track sentiment on an ongoing basis. Connections are made between the findings of the engagement and pulse surveys, as well as automated joiner and exit surveys. This allows them to identify expectation gaps and misalignment. Insights are used to develop a broader employment brand, which is linked to organisational values and leadership behaviours.

A key tool is integrated people analytics that uses a broad range of connected data. These can include unstructured qualitative data, survey results, network data, human capital data, operational and business measures, and customer feedback such as NPS. Insights are used to personalise communications. The employment brand is translated into a differentiated employee value proposition (EVP) that is customised for key talent groups.

In mature, employee-intelligent organisations, data are translated from moment-in-time insights into employee journey maps and personas. They focus on a deep understanding of cohorts and critical talent and the employee life cycle. HR takes a design-thinking approach to employee experience. This means maximising the value of key episodes and moments, such as on-boarding, anniversaries, performance reviews, development discussions, and so on. They do this through prototyping and testing, from learning what's working well and what's not, and through rapid iteration. All people managers understand their role in delivering experiences that build trust in the future.

One problem with maturity curves like this is that they are seen as a sequential progression when it's my experience that in practice things are typically messy and uneven. But by assessing where you fall in terms of your current EX capability you can identify where you need to focus and how to prioritise your efforts.

One thing that the CX expert Alan Pennington argues is that it's best to focus on lots of small changes rather than major programmes when it comes to experience management: "Your mantra for change is 100s and then 1000s of tiny changes."

This is the focus of the next chapter on putting EX into practice. It highlights the data and analytics you can use to increase your level of maturity in terms of both insights and activation. It also recommends lots of small steps, rather than trying to do everything at once.

8. EX: An Emerging Science

Employee experience is an emerging science that provides new opportunities for building trust. It's a way of analysing employee journeys, so that key touch points and processes can be improved and a lift in performance gained.

EX gives a broad and holistic view of people and organisations, but it begins by understanding individual perspectives and small moments and events. It is not a snapshot in time, but rather a series of interactions that take place over time.

This chapter explores this emerging science in more detail. It looks at new sources of EX data and new ways of generating insights. However, it's important to set out that EX does not begin with the data, but with the business questions that you need to solve.

EX is a new way of answering your key business questions, beginning with the one that is the focus of this book. Namely, how you build trust, so that people collaborate effectively and are enabled to contribute their best ideas and, in turn, deliver compelling customer experiences. Closing the trust gap in this way is an increasingly important focus for all organisations as they manage a growing tension between individual risk and human contribution in the future of work.

What is new about EX, is how you find the evidence to answer your most important business questions.

Up to now, surveys have been the key method of employee engagement programmes. While surveys will remain part of the EX tool kit, they're more likely to be pulse surveys than big, companywide surveys. And in general, organisations are going to be less reliant on surveys than in the past. This is because you can now analyse new sets of EX data. In particular, you can explore the online data that people leave behind. These are sometimes referred to as "digital breadcrumbs" and you can investigate them in an automated way in real time.

On top of this, you no longer need to rely on measuring an intervening variable like job satisfaction or engagement, which is presumed to have an impact on performance. You can now directly study behaviours and performance and the specific linkage between EX and CX.

To an extent, EX marks a return to the earliest era of employee research – before standardised engagement programmes. This is because you need to carefully establish your research question and then think about the evidence you will need to help answer it. You should be thoughtful and creative in how you go about doing that. You need to be aware of the opportunities, but also mindful of the challenges and risks.

An EX view of employee engagement

One way to illustrate the shift to employee experience in practice is to consider the EX view of employee engagement.

The traditional way to measure and improve engagement has been to conduct a survey at a point in time and to analyse the scores for teams, markets, divisions, and the company as a whole.

That score can be tracked back to a prior survey. It can be compared against benchmarks. You can analyse survey results to understand which aspects of the job are key drivers of employee engagement.

Many companies report their engagement score and categorise it as low, average or high. They judge the effectiveness of their engagement programmes by whether scores move up or down.

An EX view on employee engagement shifts away from a score to consider a dynamic formula instead. That formula looks at the change in individuals' engagement scores over time, since the moment they joined the company and across key personal milestones.

Engagement decay

This reflects the fact that engagement tends to decline over time.

In any organisation, engagement scores are highest for your newest employees. Assuming you do a reasonable job of onboarding, then people with low tenure benefit from a honeymoon effect. This arises because, through the process of joining, they have been taught about your values and your objectives, and they have consumed your internal marketing efforts. They are also probably looking for positive evidence to affirm they made the right decision in joining (this is a form of confirmation bias).

Over time, engagement declines and typically reaches a low for employees with around ten years' service. By this point, people have put in a good stint. Some are thinking it's time for a career move. They want to get rewarded for the experience they have accrued. Some are frustrated at missing out on promotion and other opportunities. Over a span of that many years, some people will feel the company has changed significantly and perhaps for the worse.

Engagement normally picks up again after this point. By then, people have elected to stay at the company longer term. They may be in more senior positions. They may also have a different deal from newer employees in terms of benefits like pensions. Sometimes these benefits can actually lock in even unhappy employees.

One simple way of looking at the overall trend in engagement, therefore, is to measure the change in the rate of decay over time. How shallow is the decline? Does engagement fall sharply? Are there points at which engagement drops off markedly? This can be visualised as a survival curve or a formula. One way to understand the effectiveness of your engagement strategy is to see if your rate of decay is slowing over time.

Survival curves and event studies

An EX perspective also zooms in on the process of decay by analysing more continuous data, especially from the early years of working at the company. Slowing the rate of decay in the early period is probably your biggest opportunity for an overall lift.

It also means examining detailed micro-maps for key talent groups specifically. What is the curve for your graduate recruits in their first 6, 12 and 18 months? You can build a micro-map for the key touch points in order to understand where you can intervene to raise engagement.

You can assess the impact of your interventions by comparing the curve for later cohorts against earlier graduate classes. Is it getting shallower? Are you managing to improve engagement and build trust at the moments that really matter? You can iterate and experiment with different interventions to compare the impact and to identify the most effective changes.

The rate of decay needs to be analysed from a systems perspective. For example, you need to consider whether changes are due to other factors. If the business is doing well, for example, you need to be able to isolate individual improvements, rather than just observing all scores rising (a halo effect).

Alternatively, perhaps the business is facing increased pressures and there is a need to reduce costs and to restructure. In this case, you need to be able to put changes over time in the context of an overall downward trend. In this scenario, standing still and maintaining a steady rate of decay can be a good result.

Survival curves are not only useful for examining engagement trends. The same approach can help in understanding turnover and attrition. Moreover, this time-based analysis (or analysis of events over time) is also critical from a diversity lens.

Take, for example, analysis of gender pay gaps. Due to the persistence of differences between men and women's pay, despite fair pay legislation, all large companies in the UK now have to report overall information on the pay gap between men and women.

The gender pay gap is the difference between the average earnings of men and women, expressed relative to men's earnings. Companies must publish on their website the mean gender pay gap, the median gender pay gap, the mean bonus gender pay gap, the median bonus gender pay gap, the proportion of males and females receiving a bonus payment, and the proportion of males and females in each pay quartile.

These are pretty crude numbers. The main idea behind reporting them is to embarrass companies into action. It is far more useful from an EX point of view, to understand how and when pay gaps develop.

Recent research, for example, has looked at the evidence of "child penalties" in female and male earnings. It's an awkward phrase, but a "child penalty" is the percentage by which women fall behind men due to having children (because of declines in labour force participation, hours of work and also wage rates). By looking at things this way, you can track differences over time and study the impact of events (such as the birth of a first child).

An international study by Henrik Kleven and others found that there are striking similarities in the qualitative effects of having children across countries, but also sharp differences in the magnitude of the effects. These differences are due to things like family policies (parental leave and child care provision) and also gender norms.

By measuring the impact of events and experiences in this way, it's possible to develop a far more useful view of how and when gender gaps develop than an aggregate point-in-time score provides. It can help in identifying policy and other options at key moments in order to create more positive outcomes.

Systems thinking

Event studies are a useful component of systems thinking, which is critical in any EX approach to employee engagement. It's best to view engagement as part of an overall system of organisational effectiveness. Engagement is the result of individual personal characteristics, workplace dynamics, management and people policies, as well as organisational performance and broader economic forces. In turn, engagement also contributes to performance and shapes factors like collaboration, effectiveness and productivity.

Systems thinking in organisational development was pioneered by writers like Peter Senge and John Sterman in the 1990s. It examines how individuals interact with the other parts of complex and dynamic systems.

Systems theory more generally has an even longer tradition, including the work of Talcott Parsons in sociology in the 1950s. Systems engineering can be traced back further, to the 1940s.

The goal of systems theory is to discover a system's dynamics, constraints, conditions and principles. It focuses on interrelationships and how changes in one part of a system impact and cause related effects elsewhere.

Two key dimensions of systems dynamics are causal loops (such as virtuous circles) and stocks and flows. Stocks are things that can either accumulate or be depleted. The most common analogy is a bathtub, which holds a volume of water. Flows are things that affect stocks, like how a drain or a tap affects the level of water in the bathtub. In a stock and flow diagram, a flow is the rate of change in a stock.

A systems view of engagement considers it a stock. It is the job of EX analytics to identify which flows reduce engagement over time and which provide an increase over time, so that you can accumulate a greater stock of engagement in your organisation.

In fact, it's possible to build a simulation, which incorporates key learnings from your employee journey maps, so you can predict and plan for engagement rising and falling in response to changes and interventions.

In this way, an EX approach to employee engagement focuses on the system dynamics of individual engagement journeys, rather than simply tracking an overall aggregate engagement score.

EX data

As described earlier in this book, most employee engagement programmes have used surveys that are sent to all employees during a single two-week window once a year.

Many companies have kept an annual survey like this as a foundational element of their employee listening strategy, even if they have shifted towards a focus on EX.

This is because they provide a way of listening to all voices: older and younger employees, office and field-based employees, manufacturing and shift workers, and so on. They are an opportunity for a broad conversation about team performance. They yield data and insights that can lead to dialogue and action. The process itself can be a means of creating engagement and involvement.

But shifting to EX means using a broader variety of data and many companies are now supplementing their annual survey with more ongoing and continuous listening.

This can include a wide range of newly available data. These can come from social platforms and productivity tools, advocacy tools, external websites, and even wearable devices. (All these sources are discussed in more detail shortly.) It can include daily or weekly polls and interactive sessions such as jams, hackathons and virtual focus groups. It can also include pulse surveys.

Pulse surveys are often shorter in length. They are sometimes only sent to a sample of the workforce. They are designed to be simple, light and fast, so you can capture feedback in the moment, on a more agile basis.

They have become very popular.

Pulse surveys at Twitter, Facebook, Amazon (and everywhere)

The most common use of pulse surveys is as a follow-up to a companywide survey, perhaps six months later. A pulse survey like this uses a subset of questions from a longer survey. Often, it will track an engagement score, as well as ask questions about action planning and communication. It will usually give space for quite a few open comments.

Pulse surveys have really taken off and become widespread in many companies. This is despite the risk of fatigue and the challenges of creating meaningful change when you only ask a few key questions. (There are also technical challenges with sampling, if you want to ensure both an accurate overall picture and useful results at a team level as well.)

The objective of a typical pulse survey is to ensure that progress is being made quickly and especially in units where engagement is low.

They are used to provide an update to leadership. If the results aren't improving, it can mean further investment in those key areas and more support for those low-engagement teams.

Quarterly pulse surveys (often with a rolling sample) have become a common feature in large banks, which operate on a tight quarter-by-quarter basis as businesses. In some cases, these replace an annual engagement survey. More commonly, they are run in addition.

This investment in running frequent surveys in banks is also the result of recent history. Following the financial crash, there have been calls for wholescale culture change inside large banks. At the same time, new corporate governance codes in the UK mean that board members are more accountable for people risks, including culture. So pulse surveys are one way of measuring whether quick progress is being made.

Some technology companies, where staff are always online, have also deployed frequent pulse surveys. For example, one company that has fully changed from a single annual survey to an ongoing pulse approach is Twitter. Their survey is run across six "windows" during the year, and is effectively always open.

In each window, one-sixth of the company's workforce is surveyed. In order to avoid fatigue, each employee is only surveyed once. Twice a year, the results are rolled up for a global view. A manager's dashboard updates throughout the year as more of their team complete the survey. The expectation is that each manager will take one action on their results when they have enough responses for a team dialogue.

The survey includes a fixed core of 15 questions, which measure things like your connection to your job, manager, team and company. Other content changes each time. And the survey is adaptive. In other words, it asks respondents to rank topics, and then, based on that ranking, employees answer items on their top themes. This is how they keep survey length as efficient as possible.

This approach is a good fit for their engineering culture. It's tempting to think of software companies as creative places, but in fact they're full of detail-orientated engineers. These are people who often like complicated and structured processes.

Another company that has deployed pulse surveys is Amazon. Every morning, Amazon employees can begin their day by answering a question that pops up on their screens. The question might ask about their team, their manager, the effectiveness of meetings, and so on. It might also ask about facilities and the work environment.

This daily poll is called Connections and it helps the People Science team at Amazon learn more about employee experiences. According to the Beth Galetti, head of HR at Amazon, "The goals are to strengthen Amazon's workplace culture and help develop leaders who earn trust, to remove barriers to excellence and to make Amazon an inspiring place to work."

According to Beth, "Connections data helped identify the three areas that make the greatest difference to employees' job satisfaction: a sense of making progress in their career, ability to use their strengths at work, and seeing work as a positive challenge."

At the same time as Amazon rolled out Connections, they also introduced a new performance feedback system called Forte. This provides more continuous feedback than the prior appraisal-based approach. It focuses on people's strengths and what they are doing well, not only areas for improvement.

Facebook is another company that runs pulse surveys. Why? For one thing, their own research has shown them that surveys are actually quite good at predicting things like employee turnover. For another, they find that employees value the chance to give their views anonymously through surveys.

Facebook runs a twice-a-year pulse survey, as well as other ad hoc surveys. They often try out new questions with different samples of people. They actually see a behavioural impact of simply asking new questions. For example, when they asked people about their own commitment to improving their experience of working at the company, then they saw an uptake in use of the tools that are available to them. (This is a form of "nudging", which is discussed in more detail later.)

According to Scott Judd, head of People Analytics at Facebook, pulse surveys are an important part of their EX tool kit, even in an age of continuous listening via social media: "Smart technology and big data will continue to help us figure out what matters most to our people. But that will make surveys more important, not less. In an age where more employees are afraid that Big Brother is watching and companies have the tools to observe more than ever before, running a survey can signal that Big Brother is still human."

This is a notable insight, coming as it does, from Facebook.

Internal social media

Pulse surveys, then, are an increasingly popular tool for collecting employee feedback, as these different examples show.

They can now also be supplemented by individual listening moments that are captured by bots running autonomously on internal social media.

There are a number of social and collaboration platforms that are becoming common in large organisations. Each has a slightly different flavour, but they all provide the opportunity to transform the way companies communicate with staff. They also open up new opportunities for capturing and using EX data.

In the technology sector, Slack is the most common platform. SLACK is actually an acronym for "Searchable Log of All Conversation and Knowledge" – which is a tantalising prospect for EX data, if you think about it.

Slack is a cloud-based set of collaboration tools and services. It allows team members to communicate through messaging and chat, and provides a community platform. Communication in Slack happens in channels, which are organised by project, topic, team, and so on. It's possible to buy or build apps to run on Slack and to integrate information and alerts from other productivity tools.

Another social collaboration platform is Workplace. This is Facebook's foray into the corporate world of work. Workplace operates just like Facebook. Departments and teams can share information via news feeds. You can get real-time feedback via likes, comments and reactions. It includes chat and video and it also integrates with apps and other tools.

A third platform is Teams (from Microsoft). MS Teams is a messaging platform that integrates with Office 365, Skype and One Drive. Microsoft looked at buying Slack in 2016, but (eventually) decided to build its own alternative instead.

These tools, along with other technologies like portals, bring the performance marketing approach that has become so prevalent in external marketing and advertising to the world of internal communications, employee engagement and employee experience.

Just as in the CX world, a rich data set is now available for EX analytics, including clicks, likes, reactions, comments, surveys, polls, and so on. It's possible to personalise communications based on analytics and to quickly iterate and then refine messages based on how people are responding.

Bot-driven data collection

It is also possible to automate data collection through the use of bots. Survey bots can run on these platforms as an app.

They can be used to run numerous kinds of polls, which can be triggered by workflows and processes. This means they're collecting individual feedback from people based on actions they have taken, events they have attended, or particular individual moments, such joining a team, the end of a project, a change of manager, and so on.

These bot surveys are usually chat based. Once programmed to run, they can collect data as a background routine, with the results analysed on an ongoing basis.

This is a new kind of data for EX analytics, which is sometimes called continuous listening. It provides the means for capturing feedback from individuals at the key moments that matter for them, so you can analyse the impact of those moments and identify ways of improving outcomes as a result.

This is in addition to the performance marketing metrics that can be also analysed in parallel.

A key advantage of this approach is personalisation. Bot surveys feel more like a conversation (or at least an online conversation) than a typical engagement survey.

Importantly, the timing can reflect moments that are relevant to employees, rather than an arbitrary two-week survey window that is chosen as a convenient time for the company.

Instead, you're giving feedback at key stages of a project, on your anniversary, a few days after a promotion, and so on. It reflects your experience. Your feedback is being captured close to the moments that matter to you.

Virtual focus groups

Sometimes, however, you need to get a deeper insight into an issue. Perhaps you're looking to understand which processes are thwarting your attempts at improving productivity? Possibly your focus is on improving your safety record, and you want to know what happens when people observe potential risks? Maybe you're considering a change to people's benefits and you want to consult with employees beforehand. These types of issues are likely to be better investigated through conversation, rather than a survey.

In the past, companies might have embarked on a series of focus groups with employees when looking at issues like these. But focus groups can be difficult to organise and expensive.

You need to manage the sampling, so that you involve a representative group of employees. This might be a mix of levels, functions and locations.

You need to make sure groups aren't being manipulated on the ground. Unions may want their reps involved. Local managers might want to avoid people with negative opinions.

There's also a cost for taking people off the line and potentially for people to travel to attend the focus groups.

The data are intensive to collect, requiring a facilitator and a note taker. After the session, the notes need to be analysed and themes synthesised. Then the findings need to be reported back in a way that makes sense.

There are big benefits to focus groups, of course. They provide rich data and insights into complex issues. They can help provide answers to problem statements. They can identify ways of fixing issues. Bringing people together also has a benefit, in terms of creating a champion network, for example.

Chat-based technology means you can now run focus groups effectively and cheaply and on a large scale.

These are sometimes called digital or virtual focus groups. Hundreds of people can participate in a single session via chat. There is normally a human moderator, but software can use algorithms to suggest follow-up questions. This can include using conjoint-type analysis to prioritise response options on the fly.

One advantage of these tools is the ability to use data science approaches to analyse responses quickly and at scale. For example, you can easily score and rank results and measure consensus. You can also segment results and look at different clusters of respondents. All of this can be done live. Results can be played back instantly.

You lose something from not having everybody in the same physical space. You cannot, for example, read the body language of people in a room. But the speed and efficiency of virtual focus groups provides a great opportunity for involving large numbers of people in deep, qualitative research like never before.

Metadata

As well as pulse surveys and feedback from continuous listening, organisations can use other data for EX analytics. One source is metadata, which come from email and calendars. Access to this information has led to a renewed interest in social network analysis in order to improve collaboration and productivity.

Social Network Analysis (SNA) has been around for a long time. Helen Jennings, for example, explored social networks in her analysis of leadership in the 1930s. It involves investigating social structures through the use of networks and graph theory. Networks are defined in terms of nodes (individuals) and the links (relationships) that connect them.

SNA measures things like density (the number of connections an individual has) and centrality (the extent to which an individual interacts with others in the network).

Sociograms or social network graphs can be used to visualise connections, mapping the structure of interpersonal relations within a group.

With the rise of Facebook and Twitter, interest in SNA has really taken off in recent years, as people look to understand online behaviour, the formation of online tribes and cliques, and the spread of information (and disinformation).

In organisational research, most social network analysis has traditionally used surveys (this is sometimes called active data collection). However, they are not easy surveys to run on a large scale, as they ask in detail about specific people and the nature of the relationship you have with them.

So surveys have often been used for relatively small groups and only on detailed projects. This might include studying collaboration in specific work spaces, such as in a Research and Development function, for example.

The new area for organisational network analysis, however, is passive data collection. This means gathering the digital trail left behind in online communications. With passive data collection, it's now possible to look at much larger organisational networks and in real time.

The leader in this field is probably Microsoft, which has built Workplace Analytics into its Office 365 suite. This allows organisations to look at email and calendar metadata (so not the content of messages and meetings, but the data that is held about the message, such as the subject line). In this way you can examine patterns of communication (who's emailing whom) and collaboration (who's meeting whom) on a large scale.

There are obviously problems with these kind of data. For example, how up-to-date is your calendar, really? But perhaps the best feature of this approach is that it can provide individuals with information about their own productivity.

Individual and team productivity

Microsoft calls this MyAnalytics, which is an app for Outlook. Based on your data, it generates a series of behavioural nudges, in other words, indirect tips. For example, the app will remind you to set aside time for focused work, before accepting a new meeting invite.

Some writers, such as Josh Bersin see this kind of approach as a natural evolution for many employee engagement programmes. Nudge theory builds on work in behavioural economics, which has become a popular approach for understanding how people really behave when presented with choices and incentives. By incorporating behavioural nudges into feedback tools, companies can help individuals to make changes that are more likely to be sustained over time.

Tools like MyAnalytics are also a response to the fact that organisations are running lean. As described earlier in this book, many companies face challenges with employee stress, well-being and burn out. By providing people with their own individual feedback, you can enable them to take action on things that benefit their own productivity and well-being.

The interest in network analysis also reflects the fact that organisations are changing shape. Traditional hierarchies are being simplified. Management layers are being removed. In some cases this is done to save money. In other cases, it is part of a hollowing-out of organisations, which is due to technology and automation.

As a result, greater emphasis is being placed on project and other teams. The rise of teams (and teams of teams) has been a slogan in organisational design for several years. This is because digital transformation often requires more flexible work structures than functionally-based (or even matrixed) organisations provide.

In practice, this means moving people into customer, product or market-focused teams. These may be short-term and temporary, containing a mix of employees and other worker types, including partners. They may be led by team leaders who are experts in their field, rather than experienced people managers. Teams may set their own goals and make their own decisions, within the context of a broader business plan, rather than follow traditional performance management routines.

SNA can be used to assess the effectiveness of these team structures, in terms of collaboration, productivity and innovation.

Another important use of SNA is in improving the effectiveness of diversity and inclusion programmes. For example, recent research into the career progression of MBA graduates using SNA has shown that for both men and women, landing top leadership positions was correlated with having high centrality in their peer network. But the researchers also found that high-placing women shared an additional characteristic, in that they had a tight-knit inner circle of other well-connected women. This kind of insight can help organisations to better shape mentoring programmes and networking events, for example.

Wearables and smart badges

SNA can also help in setting teams up to be successful in terms of physical work space.

There is a renewed focus in many organisations on the physical work space, especially offices (as we saw in the earlier case study of EX at Landsec). Office design has shifted over the years, from a mix of private offices and open plan workstations, to cubicles, and currently to large open floors, which are often broken up by communal areas and meeting spaces.

There is a blur of marketing reasons that are used to justify open-planned offices. It's relatively easy to move teams around, so you can adapt to project cycles and business changes. There's an assumption that an open floor removes barriers to collaboration. Managers sitting alongside staff, rather than in their own rooms, is seen as less hierarchical.

In fact, most research shows that working in an open-plan office reduces levels of concentration, can cause stress, affects collaboration and limits productivity. The reality is that the modern focus on open floors is largely a consequence of the high cost of real estate, especially in prime city centre locations. It's about squeezing people in.

In London, for example, the space occupied by companies has shrunk by 3 million square feet in the last three years. Looking further back, twenty years ago, each worker was allocated on average 98 square feet (this figure includes their share of communal spaces as well as individual desk space). The figure now stands at 79 square feet per worker, almost 20 per cent less. This process is sometimes called "densification".

Given these constraints, it has become important to understand the trade-offs you can make in office layout, so you can optimise different outcomes. How do you split up an open floor? Where do you need communal areas? Do you have enough break-out spaces? Are there any bottlenecks?

One way of doing this is to study how people move around and interact. In the past, this might have involved a mix of observation, surveys and focus groups. A more modern form of EX data is collected via smart badges.

Smart badges can be worn by employees on a lanyard, much like their usual security pass. The badges can track your movements, record who you're talking to and meeting with. In some cases they can also assess the tone of a conversation. (Is it loud and angry?) They can be used to study and understand patterns of interaction, so you can make adjustments to the physical environment and improve collaboration and communication.

There are clearly privacy concerns with these kind of data. As discussed later in this chapter, there are fears that a quantified work place can turn into a high-surveillance work place. Typically, in these projects, therefore, participants are required to opt in and the results are only played back at a network level.

Often the results are used in a practical way that can be seen in physical changes that are made to the office. Individuals can also be given their own feedback separately.

Data from smart badges and wearables often complement other forms of data collection, including active data collection like surveys. Badges can be especially useful for tracking behaviour over a longer, more continuous period. The most effective social network analysis, therefore, relies on combining both active and passive data together.

External data

It's not only data gathered from internal sources that are important for EX analytics. Useful data are available on external sites like Glassdoor, LinkedIn and Twitter. Other external sources of EX data include recruiters, job candidates and former employees. You can also analyse data from customers and partners.

Glassdoor was launched in 2008 and has grown rapidly. It has now collected more than 45 million reviews on over 800,000 employers. It receives more than 60 million visitors each month, making it one of the world's largest job sites.

Its original mission was to help increase workplace transparency for the benefit of both employers and employees. It is a great illustration of the overall shift that is taking place to a bottom-up approach to employee experience.

Effectively, Glassdoor provides TripAdvisor-type feedback on employers, with all the pros and cons of that kind of approach. For example, Glassdoor members self-declare their relationship to their employer (no checks are made). Glassdoor itself admits they don't know how reliable any single review is.

Most large companies now realise they need to be proactive in giving a reply to negative reviews (and responding to positive ones too). Having an effective strategy towards sites like Glassdoor is an important part of overall employer brand management. The best companies actively use external social media, not just Glassdoor, to tell stories about their company and to demonstrate their value proposition as a good place to work.

A recent Wall Street Journal report pointed out that some companies take this a step further and secretly boost their Glassdoor ratings. In these cases, companies put pressure on employees to write favourable reviews.

Studies into periods when there are spikes in the number of ratings submitted – for example, close to the announcement of Glassdoor's Best Places to Work league table – have shown that many of these reviews are suspiciously favourable (often five stars).

It's not surprising that some companies would try to game the system. Similar problems affect Amazon and TripAdvisor in the CX world.

In terms of generally how valid these data are, Glassdoor ratings (once enough have been submitted on a particular company) have been shown to correlate with internal employee engagement data. Glassdoor's overall score for employee satisfaction – 73 per cent of employees say they are satisfied at work – is also in line with other benchmarks.

Often the qualitative feedback on Glassdoor is rich, especially in terms of candidate feedback. As a result, it's become an important resource for potential recruits looking to get a sense of the candidate experience they might expect. It's also very useful data for companies looking to understand candidate perceptions of their brand and where there might be expectation gaps.

Employee advocacy

Another source of EX data are advocacy tools such as Everyone Social and LinkedIn Elevate. These tools make it easy for employees to share company content with their own social networks. This might include new product launches, new services, new research, job postings, and activities like volunteering and charitable work.

Research has shown that when it comes to corporate information, employees' own recommendations are the most trusted source of insight. But according to LinkedIn, only a very small proportion of employees (around 2 per cent) actually re-post and share company information online.

Interestingly, that 2 per cent has a strong amplifying effect. They generate around 20 per cent of the total number of views, downloads and clicks related to company information on social media.

Advocacy tools are designed to make it easy for employees to share company news. They can also help by gamifying advocacy. For example, by rewarding top advocates for sharing content.

As well as content syndication and publishing, these tools provide a means of measuring and monitoring advocacy, including identifying top influencers. In other words, you can track the take up of these tools and see which information is being shared and how. This can provide key information from a performance marketing perspective, helping you shape and refine your messaging. It also provides a measure of employee engagement.

Employee advocacy, of course, has long been measured in employee opinion surveys. Employees' willingness to recommend a company and its products are often key questions in an employee engagement index. It is seen as a measure of behavioural commitment. This is because advocacy is an activity that goes beyond the formal bounds of a traditional job. In other words, it's a behaviour that is symptomatic of going the extra mile.

In some of my clients, as well as measuring advocacy, we have also measured brand ambassadorship. This takes the concept a step further.

Imagine that you work for a food company and you're with a group of friends or associates who are discussing the obesity crisis. Are you equipped and are you willing to talk about what the company is doing to bring healthy products to the market? Or do you keep quiet or maybe try to change the topic?

Perhaps you work in the beauty industry and, walking through an airport duty-free shop one day, you notice your perfume bottles are arranged messily on the shelves. Do you walk up to the display and align the labels and then go talk to a store assistant? Or do you just walk on and head to your gate?

Maybe you work for a sports brand. Do you post selfies wearing the company's clothing and using their equipment? Do you share videos, reviews and updates with your social network? Even though companies may establish formal marketing relationships with online influencers and ambassadors, there's a big role here for employees as well.

From an employee perspective, a brand ambassador is someone who is an enthusiastic customer of their company's products and brands. They are proud of their employer and willingly communicate that pride.

More and more, as companies increasingly compete on intangibles, employees themselves are an important part of promoting, and if necessary, defending your brand. An effective approach to EX means that in key moments, employees are ready to be your company's ambassadors.

Net Promoter Scores

In employee surveys, it has become popular to measure advocacy through a Net Promoter Score (NPS). This has the benefit of being aligned to CX measurement, where NPS is a popular measure.

In CX research, you are asked to rate how likely you are to recommend a company's products and services to friends and family. In EX research, you're also asked to rate how likely you are to recommend the company as a good place to work.

NPS uses a zero-to-ten scale. Respondents who choose anywhere between zero and six, are labelled Detractors. If you choose seven or eight, you are Passive. If you choose nine or ten, you are a Promoter.

The NPS score is determined by subtracting the proportion of Detractors from the proportion of Promoters. In customer surveys, you may get a score as high as 70. In employee NPS, it's common to get lower scores. A high employee NPS score is around 35.

NPS rode to fame on the back of some impressive (Gallup-esque) marketing efforts.

It was originally designed by Fred Reichheld and others at the management consultancy Bain & Company. They wrote an article in Harvard Business Review in 2003, titled "The One Number You Need to Grow." In 2006, Reichheld followed this up with a book called *The Ultimate Question.*

Fred Reichheld is an expert on CX and customer loyalty. His book really found its market. Bain established a partnership with the research firm Satmetrix Systems in order to collect data, standardise NPS measurement, and to demonstrate its business value. NPS subsequently became very popular in customer research.

It has allowed companies to benchmark their scores. It has provided a way of aligning CX measurement across different business areas. It is also popular, in part, because the attention span of customer survey respondents is so short that you have to capture feedback very quickly. Hence, it's handy to know the one question you need to ask.

As a consequence of the growth of interest in customer NPS, and in an attempt to align measurement externally and internally, some HR departments have picked up on the concept. They have applied it to employee insights in order to measure employee loyalty and advocacy.

Some organisations have entirely replaced their employee engagement survey with a short employee NPS survey instead. Others have added an NPS question to their existing surveys.

For some stakeholders, like sales and marketing leaders, it's a familiar measure. This can help to win their support for a company's overall employee engagement programme. For direct sales staff, for example in a call centre, it also provides a way of comparing both customer and employee NPS in order to conduct a gap analysis.

However, there are some notable problems with applying NPS to employee insights.

For one thing, the concept of loyalty and advocacy is different for employees than for customers. Employment is a deeper, longer-term, and more complicated relationship than the typical customer or consumer relationship is.

In addition, a customer purchase provides direct value to your business. But an employee's action is typically part of a long value chain, which makes it hard to suppose direct impact in the same way.

There are also technical worries about NPS when used in employee research. Some studies have shown that employee NPS is volatile over time. This is my experience as well. It's probably the case that any single-question measure tends to be less reliable than a properly developed scale of several questions.

Furthermore, NPS responses aren't normally distributed, which means you have to be careful when running additional analysis. Using the NPS scoring technique also means that a lot of information is actually discarded (all the Passive responses, for example).

The one question?

The great attraction of NPS from an EX perspective is that it provides a simple "dipstick" that you can use in all your continuous listening activities and surveys.

You need a simple and consistent measure like this, in order to track journeys and experiences over time. It's very handy, therefore, to only need one question for that. It's a big plus that NPS is already aligned to how you probably measure CX.

Given the concerns over the effectiveness of NPS, what is an alternative EX measure?

Some consulting firms have started to use a generic question like, "How positive was your experience?" But this suffers from being vague. It also continues to rely on a single measure of experience.

The better answer is a harder one: Your measure should depend on the business problems that you're looking to solve through your EX programme. For example, it might take the form of a short engagement index, if improving engagement is your aim. It might include questions measuring collaboration, empowerment or customer service.

Tracey Maylett recommends capturing employee experience across key moments by measuring elements like meaning, autonomy, growth, impact and connection. EX depends on gauging both perceptions and expectations. Consistent measurement means you can understand where you have expectation gaps.

Jacob Morgan recommends measuring an overall employee experience index score by asking about three key aspects: culture, technology and physical space.

Based on his research, he estimates that only the top 5 per cent of companies are really successful EX organisations, which he calls "Experiential". By this he means "they are doing an amazing job of investing in and designing for these three environments."

In the CX world, Alan Pennington argues that NPS is more about the direction of travel than the actual result. He thinks it's more useful to capture customer effort instead. This is because reducing customer effort improves loyalty.

Such a question might be along the lines of "How much effort did you have to put forth to handle your request?" In an EX world the question might be, "How much effort was required to achieve your goal?"

Beyond effort, it is also useful to capture an expectation score, along the lines of "Failing to meet your expectations" – "Meeting your expectations" – "Exceeding your expectations". This kind of measurement needs to be captured in the moment, so that the respondent is able to recall events without any difficulty.

In this way, you can then compare effort (or satisfaction) and delivery (beating expectations) in order to prioritise focus areas. In these cases, it's important to capture qualitative feedback at the same time.

The best EX questions are those that you have connected to performance outcomes in your own business. This can be done through linkage research, such as a service profit chain analysis described in earlier chapters.

Your EX measure should then comprise a short number of these critical and consistent items. This is far more useful than general, overall statements.

In an EX world, these measurement problems can also be partly solved by looking directly at behaviour by analysing the data collected though online social tools. If this isn't a replacement, it can be certainly be an effective complement or a means of triangulation.

This illustrates an important difference between an EX approach and traditional employee research. Previously, you had to ask about intentions and behaviours in surveys and then make sense of the responses you got back. You created an intervening variable like engagement in order to link opinions to performance.

Now, in terms of advocacy, for example, you can look directly at what people share, with whom, and how.

You can also try different approaches, in terms of providing access to information, and then iterate those approaches in order to optimise take-up. You can analyse trends in real time to see if you're being successful.

This is the data science approach to EX analytics, which, with the adoption of new social technologies, is beginning to take off.

It's not just advocacy where this can be deployed. Similar approaches can be used in understanding turnover risks.

Employee retention

Employee turnover is a real concern for a lot of organisations.

Some skills are in short supply and high demand. Digital skills – including artificial intelligence and data systems – fall into this category, for example. It can be hard to attract and then retain people with these "hot" skills.

In Western Europe, there is a demographic bulge heading into retirement age. They are potentially taking a lot of experience and knowledge with them. So it's important to understand how to retain people with key skills and to transfer their knowledge.

There is also a more general awareness that it's important to retain your best performers. According to some research, top performers can produce 20 to 30 times more than the "average employee" in their fields.

Moreover, there is a clear business case for focusing on retention. The cost of voluntary turnover (when employees willingly choose to leave their positions) is significant. Deloitte estimates that the cost of losing an employee can range from tens of thousands of dollars to two times the employee's annual salary.

The costs include hiring, on-boarding, training, the time it takes to reach peak productivity, the loss of engagement from others due to high turnover, higher business error rates, and general impacts on the work culture.

For all these reasons, there is an increased focus on holding on to your most important employees.

One way of understanding how to minimise turnover is to build a model. This can be based on a review of turnover data, insights from surveys and qualitative feedback (for example, from exit interviews).

Most engagement surveys include some kind of measure of retention, such as a stated intention to stay or leave over the next year. Important drivers may include things like job flexibility, opportunities for learning and advancement, relationship with your manager and team mates, and so on.

Other retention factors might include individual variables such as time since last promotion and pay rate compared to co-workers, and so on. They might also include data on fitness for the job at the point of hire.

A common approach is to use all these aspects to model employee attrition. With bigger and better data sets, some companies now use machine learning (such as random forests and ensemble methods) in order to get better predictive performance.

In an EX world, it's also possible to add direct behaviours to this analysis.

IBM, for example, claims that its predictive attrition algorithm can predict "with 95 per cent accuracy" employees who are likely to leave in the next six months. Their model includes thousands of pieces of data. It is then set up to nudge managers, so they can pay attention to team members who may be on their way out (as long as they're valued employees, of course).

Some companies have built attrition models which include analysis of email and calendar metadata. Network analysis, for example, has shown that people who are planning to leave become far less active in their internal email communications up to six months beforehand. Early signals like this can be built into your model, so you can build strategies for retaining employees who are potentially at risk of leaving.

Some tools claim to be able to index information that is also available on external social media. You can see how, for example, information about employees updating their profiles and making themselves open to approaches from recruiters is a useful addition to any predictive algorithm.

It's another emerging data science approach to EX: learning from employee journeys, building a predictive model, examining actual behaviours, highlighting areas of turnover risk, and nudging managers to take action.

Problems with individual EX data

This kind of analysis obviously raises questions about who owns what data, where the boundary between personal data and public data lies, and how to avoid people analytics becoming, well, creepy.

The aim of EX, after all, is to help build trust inside organisations, not to damage it.

There are some golden rules for using any kind of EX data in a positive and constructive way and in order to build trust.

The first rule is that individual experiences need to be aggregated and anonymised. In other words, it is best to analyse EX data for groups. In a traditional engagement survey, a group means a department or a business unit or a function. In EX analysis this is more likely to mean a cohort, a persona, a class, a team or a critical talent segment.

In order to preserve trust and allow people to give honest feedback the smallest size of group that you will analyse should be fixed and communicated. In employee surveys, it used to be that a group of ten respondents was an industry standard. In companies with smaller, more agile teams and an appetite for more local feedback, the group size might be as low as five. But this approach to grouping individual feedback remains the core method for protecting individual identities.

There is a growing debate over the use of anonymous feedback. Some people have argued that anonymity allows some respondents to game the system, providing skewed feedback to drive a particular result. Direct feedback, it's argued, gives more accountability and creates more openness.

In my experience, very few organisations have such a strong feedback culture and high trust levels that they're able to do this. So it's generally important to keep EX analytics anonymous and to make sure you're getting useful insights. It's worth noting that companies such as Google, Facebook and Twitter, who all handle a lot of individual and personal data, all maintain an anonymous employee survey as part of their listening approach.

But it's also important to have some direct individual feedback in your overall mix of listening strategies. This may take the form of developmental feedback for managers and team leaders, for example through a structured 360 survey process. There are also ways of providing individual feedback directly to associates (which is discussed in the final chapter).

Openness and transparency

The second golden rule is that companies need to be open about the data they collect and how they are used. People are more conscious now than ever of how their personal data can be used and misused. This is one reason why there has been pressure for regulations like the GDPR.

Employees need to opt in and give their consent. To do this in an informed way, you need to explain how and why data analysis is important. This cannot be done via a blanket approach. You need to be as specific as possible. Some companies are also exploring ways of "co-owning" the data with employees by putting data management tools in employees' hands.

The third rule is that there needs to be a defined value for individuals themselves. It needs to be clear What's In It For Me. People increasingly expect benefits in return for providing their data. For individual EX data at work this might include personalised learning, improved personal productivity, a safer work environment, fairer performance appraisals, and so on.

According to research by Accenture, 71 per cent of employees say they will only be willing to let their employer collect data on them if their employer communicates how their data will be used and the benefits they will receive.

There needs to be clear governance around individual EX data, which involves executive oversight and a clear set of checks and balances. Organisations are creating new roles such as a Chief Data Officer, to oversee areas such as data availability, transparency, quality and control.

There needs to be an awareness of how your approach to EX data aligns to your organisational values. In multinational organisations, this needs to take account of the fact that different national cultures have different attitudes to workforce data and technology. Ultimately, your values provide the framework for making decisions about EX data and analytics.

Listening versus surveillance

Great care needs to be taken in using new sources of data and new technologies as the potential for damaging trust is significant. It's sometimes hard for companies to judge exactly where the line is.

For example, when The Telegraph newspaper in the UK introduced desk monitoring devices to study how office space was being used, it led to an outcry: "One journalist called the roll out "ridiculous" and "embarrassing"; another said that "a lack of disclosure" about the devices' purpose had triggered protests." By the time the company cancelled the programme and took out the devices, many staff had already removed the batteries powering the units.

Desk monitors are actually a common feature in offices that have hot desking, so the problem in this case was more related to employee relations, communications and buy in.

Things become more complicated when monitoring activities become routinized and automated.

In call centres, companies now routinely use AI to analyse conversations. These systems can track customer sentiment (is the customer angry?) as well as how the call centre rep is being perceived (are they seen as helpful?) The benefit of these systems is that they can be used to give developmental feedback to individual workers on how to improve their interactions. As such, they can both improve individual employee experience and customer experience.

Many companies' IT departments now use advanced analytics to automatically identify deviations from normal employee digital behaviour. Basically, these programmes develop a profile based on an individual's regular routines. This means that when there is a change in behaviour, security teams can identify threats and other issues before they become serious. The benefit here for the organisation is to reduce the human element of cyber risk. Individuals may also get more tailored communication about cyber threats as a result.

Casinos have been using video and facial recognition software for some time, to spot fraud and cheating. That technology can also be used on staff: for example, by looking at interactions between dealers and gamblers. In the UK, there is some legislation that governs how you can monitor staff, but the use of facial recognition software is a growing trend. For example, there is much interest in the Western press in how it is used in China for surveillance, along with the use of social credit systems, whereby citizens' financial and social reputation is ranked.

All of this is to underline that there are clear privacy concerns over how human interactions are tracked. This is especially the case at work.

I personally have grave concerns about the use of technology and analytics for surveillance at work in the future. Some companies still have a management mindset of command and control. Some leaders prioritise the pursuit of profit above everything. Others always put cutting costs at the top of their agenda. Many organisations only pay lip service to values and behaviours. In these workplaces, there is a danger of what The Economist calls, a new digital Taylorism.

Taylorism refers to scientific management in the nineteenth century, which required a high level of managerial control over employee work practices. Digital Taylorism means using new technology to maximise efficiency through standardising tasks and routines, and using surveillance technology to monitor workers to make sure they are following those rules exactly as directed.

There is very clearly a potential dark side to the quantified workplace. In the wrong work cultures, technology and analytics could lead to a dehumanised and controlling environment. I fear for organisations that follow this path (and for the people who work in them).

The main point here, for EX measurement in general, is that the trust stakes are high. Individual experiential data always need to be treated carefully. Communication and buy-in are key. It has to be clear what the business question is and what the benefits are for the individuals involved.

These concerns highlight the final EX success factor, which is the importance of taking small steps, and piloting, testing and iterating. A critical element here is co-creation. An EX team cannot work in isolation, separate from the rest of the company, in some kind of people analytics lab where solutions are pushed from the centre out into the business.

In fact, employee involvement and discussion are crucial in order to make sure that changes offer benefits to everyone. It's also essential in order to avoid bias and unfairness in the design and use of new technologies and systems. EX is about creating conversation and dialogue, rather than surveillance and control.

Activating EX insights

In all of the above, it should be clear that EX data are harder to manage than traditional engagement survey data.

For sure, this a key reason why many companies are still running annual engagement surveys. Engagement surveys are controlled and relatively simple. An engagement survey gives you a score, which you can report, track and benchmark. These are all things that business leaders like.

By contrast, EX measurement is often less structured. There's no one number. There's a lot of testing and learning. The data sit in different pots – and sometimes those pots are even external to the organisation and outside of your control. There are exciting opportunities, but there are risks too.

Many companies visualise employee engagement as a number, a score, a bar graph or even a thermometer. There are actually a lot of medical analogies for engagement – it's a temperature, a pulse, a measure of your organisation's health.

You get your engagement score once or maybe a few times a year. The survey is a check-up, an X-ray, a moment in time. Typically, your engagement score is delivered in a PowerPoint presentation or a written report.

Rather than a medical check-up, EX is like wearing a health and activity tracker like a Fitbit. In terms of reaching your fitness goals as an organisation, EX is about tracking your vital activity as it happens. This means you can stay fit, stay motivated, and see how small steps make a big impact.

A Fitbit is a good analogy for another reason, in that there are benefits to an individual from their Fitbit data, but would you want to share all that with your employer or your health insurer? With EX data, there needs to an alignment of needs and benefits. Both employees and organisations need to benefit from EX insights.

Rather than a presentation or a report, you're more likely to visualise EX through a dashboard. That dashboard pulls in insights from different places. It shows different journeys, probably as line graphs and curves. These show the impacts over time of different interventions on critical cohorts and on business performance.

Through your dashboard, you're tracking the progress that you're making continuously. Data are updating in something like real time.

You review your EX dashboard as you make business decisions. You look to understand the impact of those decisions on key personas, moments and processes. You focus on the behaviour changes that you want to create and sustain.

The key skills here are data integration and visualisation. Rather than PowerPoint, you're more likely to use business intelligence software like Tableau or Microsoft BI.

An engagement mindset is like an audit. You're reviewing scores to see if they have gone up and down. An EX mindset is about curating experiences. It's about making adjustments to processes and systems in the moments that matter as and when they occur for groups of people as they progress through the organisation.

This is the key lens on activating EX insights. An engagement survey will lead to focus areas and action plans. EX activation refers to how you achieve your business goals through your people strategy.

It's not about creating one-off plans, but about how you better articulate, personalise and deliver your value proposition.

It's about how you use ongoing insights from employees to change processes and systems for the better. Not only in order to improve commitment, but so you can simplify the work and create a more agile and resilient organisation.

What's most critical in this activation process, of course, is leadership, which is why it is the focus of the final chapters.

9. EX Leadership

This book has taken a long-term view of the evolving field of employee experience.

It began by reviewing the major forces that are leading to a transformation of the workplace, such as automation, globalisation and demographic changes.

It moved on to look at the importance of trust to effective organisations and the existence of a damaging trust gap in many companies.

Then it reviewed how upward feedback and listening to employees – making it safe to speak up – is a critical capability for building trust.

It showed how many companies have looked to do that by capturing employee voice through surveys, engagement programmes and now employee experience.

What is common across all these pieces is the importance of leadership.

Leaders have to focus their organisations on meeting customers' needs and wants, and provide a strategy for business success. Internally, they have to translate that strategy into effective organisations and compelling jobs.

Leaders have to build trust by challenging their own perceptions and by opening themselves up to feedback.

Leaders are the key ingredient in any employee engagement programme. They are also the critical piece in the employee experience jigsaw.

For this reason, leadership is the focus of the final two chapters of this book. In them, I examine the role of leaders in driving a successful focus on EX in order to build trust and to create a high performance organisation.

EX leadership refers to two related things.

Firstly, it highlights the key role that leaders have in building engagement and a compelling employee experience.

Secondly, it highlights how some companies that are high in the EX maturity curve are pushing the boundaries and leading this emerging new science. In particular, it looks at how they use smart technology and analytics to activate their approach to employee experience.

Refreshing Coca-Cola

Over the last twenty years, I have been lucky enough to observe some great leaders up close. It's probably not advisable to highlight individuals, but some people do stand out for me.

Neville Isdell, for example, took over the reins at The Coca-Cola Company at a very difficult time. The roots of the problems lay in previous botched leadership transitions.

In 1997, Roberto Goizueta had passed away suddenly. He was a charismatic CEO who led an era of tremendous growth. But he drove that growth through his own personal discipline and networks, rather than by building a high degree of organisational discipline.

Doug Ivester became CEO after Goizueta, but this period, following such a golden era for the company, was not a successful one. By the time Ivester was replaced by Doug Daft, the company was facing rapidly changing consumer demands and growing financial pressures.

Under Daft, the company lost some of its cohesion. There was also a major split in the board, regarding the future focus for the company. The board was ruled over by Don Keough, who had been Goizueta's number two for more than ten years.

If this sounds like a soap opera, then that's not inaccurate.

According to a *Fortune* report at the time, "This is a story of byzantine manoeuvrings and warring tribes, of spin and counter-spin, of old grudges and character assassinations. The tale is long on thwarted ambitions and short on real strategy. It is positively Shakespearean."

Under Goizueta, there had been a remarkable run of success. There was a 16-year increase in the company's value that made a lot of investors rich. By 2004, the wheels were coming off.

Into this mix, Neville Isdell was persuaded to return to the company. He had had a long career in the Coca-Cola system. But having been passed over in these previous CEO successions, he had retired very comfortably to the Caribbean in 2001.

According to reports, he did have to be persuaded to come back.

As he said himself, "I really didn't want to do it. Why would I? I had the money I needed, a great retirement, a good marriage. Why would I want to wreck all of that? But that was the wrong question. The real question was how could I say no to the ultimate challenge? Not many people get the chance to run the world's biggest brand."

The chances of failure were high. As well as poor financial performance, the company faced a series of crises, including an investigation by the US Securities and Exchange Commission for alleged deceptive marketing practices. Moreover, with concerns over obesity, the carbonated beverage market was under severe focus. Consumer preferences were changing rapidly.

As described early on in this book, his ability to open up the whole organisation to difficult and challenging feedback led to a wholesale transformation of the business and a new manifesto for growth.

Ultimately, Neville was the right person, in the right place, at the right time to drive a wholesale transformation. He was completely committed to rebuilding a long-term future for The Coca-Cola Company.

He found that he enjoyed fixing the mess. In his own words, again, "I discovered within myself that is what I enjoy. I am not a good status quo manager. I get bored. I am not a good bureaucrat."

Virgin Money Giving

Jayne-Anne Ghadia is another leader who comes to mind. A Chartered Accountant by background, she worked at Norwich Union before becoming one of the founders of Virgin Direct in 1995.

In 1998 she set up the Virgin One account which was acquired by the Royal Bank of Scotland (RBS) in 2001. After five years at RBS – during its glory years under Fred "The Shred" Goodwin – she returned to Virgin as the CEO of Virgin Money.

In 2012, Virgin Money acquired crisis-stricken Northern Rock and two years later successfully listed on the London Stock Exchange.

These were tumultuous times to be a leader in the financial services sector. It was a period when many people's values were challenged.

One learning that she took from her time at RBS was the importance of diversity. According to her autobiography, a key reason for the downfall of RBS in 2008 was "the complete lack of diversity at the top of the organisation." A second key reason was a problem of leadership hubris, "Many senior managers really did believe they were Masters of the Universe."

As a result, when I worked with Jayne-Anne at Virgin Money, her commitment to using employee insights to puncture leadership assumptions and to build a culture of inclusion and diversity was second to none.

Under her leadership, Virgin Money also had a commitment, or a philosophy, that it called Everyone Better Off (EBO).

According to Jayne-Anne, "We aim to make everyone better off – to not just do the best things for our shareholders, staff, local communities and customers – but for all of them together because, in my view, if you can create a holistic approach to business you get a better outcome and more success."

A good example of this is the way the company took up sponsorship of the London Marathon and built Virgin Money Giving to collect charitable donations on a not-for-profit basis.

Internally, Virgin Money also did things like an award programme that recognised colleagues who brought EBO to life in a special and impactful way. "EBO Stars" were ambassadors for the EBO way of thinking and working. Jayne-Anne sums up this overall ethos as "Who Cares Wins".

Externally, Jayne-Anne has also been a vocal supporter of corporate social responsibility. In 2015, she led a UK government review focused on the representation of women in the Financial Services industry. Her report led to the UK Treasury's Women in Finance Charter. This is a commitment by firms to work together for gender equality in financial services.

Sustainability and transparency at SC Johnson

Fisk Johnson is a third and (again) quite different example. Fisk is the fifth generation of his family to lead SC Johnson, the consumer goods company that is headquartered in the small town of Racine in Wisconsin. He became CEO in 2004.

SC Johnson is a private company owned by the Johnson family. In fact, it's one of the oldest family-owned businesses in the USA.

The company began life in 1886, making floor products, most famously Johnson Wax. Now it's a diversified multinational, producing goods for home cleaning, home storage, air care, personal care and insect control. Its well-known brands include Glade, Raid, Pledge, and Ziploc. It has 13,000 employees across 70 countries.

In my experience, the company is pretty unique. It is genuinely a values-led company. It has always made a play of this in its consumer advertising by using the prominent tagline: "A Family Company". Internally, the company's core values were formalised by CEO Sam Johnson in 1976 in a document called *This We Believe*.

This document is still referred to today. It focuses on building trust with five key groups. The list always begins with employees, and also includes consumers, the public, local communities, and the world community at large.

According to Fisk, "*This We Believe* still provides a sounding board against which we can test ideas and consider options, and a true north from which we will not waver. Being a family company enables us to uphold its aspirations as few other organisations can."

Apart from the crucial fact of being the great-great-grandson of the company founder, Fisk has an unusual profile for a CEO. He has a PhD in Physics. He is the inventor and holder of a couple of patents. He is also passionate about conservation and sustainability.

Like all companies, SC Johnson has had to deal with waves of change and transformation over the last decade or so, but unlike some of the other examples mentioned in this book, it hasn't faced a deep crisis.

In fact, the focus at SC Johnson is more about how to best preserve the company's mission and purpose, so that it can continue to make a positive contributions to families, communities and the environment (with all the difficulties that implies for a chemicals and plastics company).

The company, under Fisk's leadership, has continued to navigate its own path, according to its own values, in a world that is impacted by climate change and environmental pressures. The goal is always to balance short- and long-term demands, and to meet family, local and global community concerns.

In terms of sustainability, SC Johnson led the way on phasing out ozone-depleting chlorofluorocarbons, minimising manufacturing waste, on powering its plants with renewable energy, and introducing plastics recycling.

SC Johnson has also pioneered transparency regarding its products. This includes its Greenlist programme, which evaluates each product ingredient for its potential impact on human health and the environment.

According to Fisk, "We view transparency as it relates to our ingredients as one important way we continue to build and maintain trust in our company and our brands."

The company is also very mindful about how it listens to its workforce and involves them in initiatives. I worked with Fisk and his team to build a new approach to employee listening in 2006.

There are some key things the company prioritises when it comes to its people, such as involvement, mutual respect and shared goals.

Above all, what is most critical, is transparency. This, again, is enshrined in their values, "Creating a climate whereby all employees freely air their concerns and express opinions with assurance that these will be fairly considered."

Leadership as service

These examples highlight some key leadership characteristics.

First among these is thinking of leadership as service, which is sometimes called servant leadership. In this case, leaders see themselves as stewards of the organisation they head. As stewards, they think about the big picture. They make decisions based on what's important to the company's long-term success.

Jim Collins and Jerry Porras (in *Built to Last*) refer to this as "clock building", which is an analogy I have always liked. "Having a great idea or being a charismatic visionary leader is time telling; building a company that can prosper far beyond the presence of any single leader and through multiple product life cycles is clock building."

Accordingly, "The primary output of their efforts is not the tangible implementation of a great idea, the expression of a charismatic personality, the gratification of their ego, or the accumulation of personal wealth. Their greatest creation is the company itself and what it stands for."

Servant leaders have an especially strong focus on ensuring that the decisions they make are aligned with the organisation's core values. The values provide a clear and practical framework for both strategic and day-to-day decision making. In addition, rather than focusing on performance directly, they focus on enabling others to be successful instead.

Obliquity

This links to a second key leadership characteristic, which is the ability to find an indirect approach to achieving your goals. The

British economist John Kay calls this "obliquity". He identifies, for example, the issue of what he calls the "profit-seeking paradox". By this he means that the most profitable companies are not actually the most profit-oriented. His conclusion is that, rather than focusing directly on profit, it's better to focus on your own big idea, commitment, ethos or sense of purpose.

Effectively, this is a critique of the behaviour of large banks ahead of the Financial Crash of 2008. John Kay argues that, "The motives that make for success in business are commitment to, and passion for that business, which is not at all the same as love of money."

To think obliquely is an especially useful way of making decisions when times are volatile, uncertain, and imperfectly understood. In crude terms, it might be described as muddling through.

According to John Kay, "Obliquity is a process of experiment and discovery. Successes and failures and the expansion of knowledge lead to reassessment of our objectives and goals and the actions that result."

As such, it's a pretty humble approach to leadership thinking. It begins by recognising that you don't have all the answers yourself.

In my experience, this is something that many leaders struggle with. Indeed, they feel they've been promoted because they're meant to be good at coming up with answers.

Reflection

A third key element of successful leaders is making time for reflection. A lot has been written about reflective leadership, much of which comes from positive psychology and emphasises the importance of understanding and leveraging your strengths as a leader.

For me, the most important elements of reflection are an openness to feedback and a curiosity to understand what it's really like for the people who work for you. In other words, a reflective leader is keen to understand the employee experience through listening, walking around and talking to people, as well as through surveys and analytics.

In the midst of these conversations, effective leaders are able to consider what it means for their role and their behaviour as a leader. For some, this is a natural way of thinking and working, but for others it requires a lot of effort.

Reflection, therefore, is a conscious process of asking important questions and internalising the feedback. It leads to a focused effort to practice the desired behaviours and to hold others to account for following a similar process.

Leaders who are not reflective tend to be narrow in their thinking and wrapped up in their own world and their own problems. They are vulnerable to hubris as a result.

EX leadership dimensions

These characteristics – service, obliquity and reflection – are a reason why I like to use collaborative models from the performance arts, such as the movie director, the stage director or the jazz ensemble, when discussing leadership practices.

In these cases, leaders are generally off-stage, worrying about the big picture. They have to be collaborative. They focus on how to get people and groups to perform at their best.

As well as these stories and observations, I have kept track of employees' perceptions of leaders' effectiveness through the different employee surveys I have been involved in.

These records go back over twenty years. They include more than 100 companies, primarily large, international, complex organisations.

I have also kept track of what the changes these companies make after employee surveys and the impact those changes have on people and performance.

So what is it specifically about EX leadership that stands out?

There are three key dimensions: purpose, learning and personalisation.

1. EX is about purpose and meaning at work

Effective leaders work hard to translate strategy and objectives into meaningful work and jobs that provide a sense of purpose. EX leadership is about giving organisations and individuals an answer to the question of "why we do this work."

To my mind, this is less about things like company mission statements. It's more about building line of sight to customers and giving employees the authority to make small changes, so they can have some impact on the sense of meaning they themselves get from their jobs.

Barry Schwartz points out in his book *Why We Work* that people get a sense of fulfilment from the work challenge, from social interaction, and from having some control over what they do. Another important factor is finding that what you do is meaningful. One important way of finding meaning is by linking what you do in your job to the welfare of others.

In some professions, such as healthcare or teaching, which are often thought of as vocations, that link to the welfare of others is clear and obvious. But in many jobs it isn't. So effective leaders inspire employees by making it clear how their job affects others in positive ways.

A common way of doing this, which is looked at in more detail below, is by building a very clear line of sight to the experience of customers. Another way of doing this is by building a strong link to the organisation's mission and vision.

Jeffrey Pfeffer makes this same observation in his book *The Human Equation*. For Pfeffer, the best companies place a great emphasis on communicating the company's mission and vision, especially as it relates to financial and business performance. In other words, they always put business success within the context of the organisation's purpose.

From the viewpoint of behavioural economics, Dan Ariely in his book *Payoff* highlights the complexity of motivation, suggesting that if you wrote down an equation to capture why you work, it would include a very long list of factors, including money, achievement, happiness, a sense of progress, security, legacy, status, and so on.

Ariely criticises many organisations for being stuck in "a factory mode of production" when it comes to thinking about motivation. By this he means that leaders focus on financial rewards for piece work, whilst they neglect fundamental social elements such as identity, goodwill, connection and meaning.

For Ariely, "We're much more driven by all kinds of intangible, emotional forces: the need to be recognised and to feel ownership; to feel a sense of accomplishment; to find the security of a long-term commitment and a sense of shared purpose. We want to feel as if our labour and lives matter in some way."

Daniel Pink, in his best-selling book *Drive*, highlights the importance of mastery and purpose in motivating people to perform at their best, which he characterises as a state of flow. More specifically, he argues that it is the pursuit of mastery that is the most important thing. Pursuit is really a mindset focused on continuous improvement and perseverance towards long-term goals (sometimes called "grit").

Accordingly, when it comes to inspiring leadership, organisations need to focus on what he calls "purpose maximisation". Successful companies do not chase profit while trying to stay ethical and values-based. Their goal is to pursue purpose and to use profit as the catalyst rather than the objective.

Daniel Pink sets out an evolution in terms of organisations' focus on motivation, from carrot and stick approaches, to performance-contingent rewards, which is where most organisations still are today, and on to what he calls Motivation 3.0: "The science shows that the secret to high performance isn't our biological drive or our reward-and-punishment drive, but our third drive – our deep-seated desire to direct our own lives, to extend and expand our abilities, and to live a life of purpose."

Daniel Pink notes, rather sadly, that the gap between what science knows and what business does is wide and it is not narrowing.

You can see this gap in the data collected in employee surveys. Most companies have a long way to go. In the UK, for example, only

56 per cent of employees say that leaders provide a vision for their company that is inspiring.

Narrowing this gap is where EX leadership really comes into play. The observation that purpose and meaning at work matters to people and performance is hardly new. What differentiates the best companies is that they actually put it into practice. That practical application is achieved through an EX lens. Overall, they are framing organisational performance in terms of individual experiences. They use EX analytics to ensure they are doing a number of important things well.

Job crafting

For example, when it comes to defining jobs, EX leaders have a focus on encouraging what is sometimes called job crafting.

In job crafting, managers provide employees with the authority and space to alter their jobs in such a way as to better suit their skills and interests. In this way, employees are able to make small, but meaningful changes to the scope of their work, and to focus especially on the purpose of their role.

As described by Justin Berg, Jane Dutton, and Amy Wrzesniewski, "Within a formally designated job, employees are often motivated to customise their jobs to better fit their motives, strengths, and passions. Job crafting is a means of describing the ways in which employees utilise opportunities to customise their jobs by actively changing their tasks and interactions with others at work."

This might mean people taking on more or fewer or different tasks, expanding or reducing the scope of tasks, or changing how they perform tasks and how they interact with others.

Arnold Bakker has looked at job crafting within the framework of job demands and resources. His research, which often involves detailed diary studies, has looked at different industries, including mining, manufacturing, healthcare and teaching. He sees job crafting as activating a virtuous cycle of employee engagement, positive team behaviours and improved job performance.

Although they're not described in the same terms, there are elements of job crafting (or dynamic work design as it is sometimes called) in the lean methodologies that have transformed the experience of working in manufacturing, and especially car making. One of the very early pioneers of these approaches was Toyota.

The Toyota Production System (TPS) was originally established by the founder of Toyota, Sakichi Toyoda and his son Kiichiro Toyoda and the engineer Taiichi Ohno who was chief of production in the post-World War Two period. The core elements of the TPS are also embedded in the company's principles and behaviours, The Toyota Way, so they are at the very heart of the way the company works and how it treats its employees.

The main goal of the TPS is to eradicate inefficiency in the production process. This means tackling the three interrelated "enemies" of working in a lean way: reducing waste (muda), minimising inconsistency (mura) and avoiding "overburden" (muri).

Two key pillars of the TPS are "just in time" (in other words, making only what is needed when it is needed) and "jidoka" which means "automation with a human touch".

The human element is a critical part of The Toyota Way, which emphasises the importance of teamwork. In fact, trust and speaking up are at the heart of lean manufacturing like this. Continuous improvement in this manner depends on key concepts such as challenge and "kaizen" (taking responsibility for driving innovation).

In plants that use these methodologies, which are very widespread today, the operator is placed at the centre of how you think about jobs. This means that the work space and work processes are all designed around providing support to operators and teams on the plant floor.

In this way, lean methodologies, which are not restricted to manufacturing, focus on aspects like autonomy, team working and skills use.

Whether you refer to it as lean manufacturing or dynamic work design or job crafting, all of these terms refer to an effective leadership style that places the employee at the heart of work arrangements and that encourages people to make small changes to improve performance.

EX and CX alignment

Another element in providing meaning and purpose is through alignment to the organisation's mission, vision and values. In practice this means that, when it comes to communication, leaders constantly link decisions and plans to the mission and vision. And when it comes to discussing behaviours, the organisation's values provide the consistent framework that is used for driving accountability and for recognising success.

Above all else, it means that EX leaders ensure there is a clear alignment between employee experience and customer experience (EX and CX).

For all organisations, your employee experience is at the heart of delivering outstanding customer experiences. Put plainly, it's not possible to deliver a simple and effective customer experience if your internal tools are clunky and hard to use. It's not possible to deliver customer delight if the people dealing with your customers are not engaged. It's impossible to provide great service if your employees are unable to exercise their own judgement effectively.

A successful customer experience strategy is the result of your company's culture. How you interact internally within your company will have an impact on external interactions too. As a result, leading companies realise that they have to focus on employees first when they try to improve their customer experience.

A positive customer experience is, of course, the responsibility of everyone in the company. But an EX lens can be deployed the most effectively at the points of intersection with your customers: sales reps, success managers, call centres, front-line staff, and so on.

In practice, this can mean linking EX and CX feedback to identify important differences and gaps, and then addressing them.

The single best way to improve both EX and CX is to improve the flow of knowledge. Too often, critical knowledge becomes stuck inside different departments, which act as silos. A key task of EX leadership is to break these silos down and to ensure that information is available to all who need it.

EX at Airbnb

One company that focuses on EX leadership at the employee-customer interface is the online hospitality company Airbnb. In practice, what do they do? Firstly, they work to integrate the company's values into all their core processes. For example, the early employee experience begins at the interview stage, which includes screening prospective candidates for hospitality and service orientation (two core values).

Then, as part of the on-boarding experience, new employees shadow current support staff for a period of time, so they get to understand the challenges that guests and hosts face.

As employees, they are expected to stay in Airbnb properties when they travel and they are also encouraged to serve as hosts, so that they experience the customer side of interactions directly.

Employees also attend company-organised events with hosts, so they can continue to understand the issues that hosts and guests face.

In all of this, Airbnb is embedding critical customer interactions through a series of key moments that matter to the employee journey. These events and experiences build overall alignment as well as individual engagement.

Experience management at Adobe

Another example is Adobe. There, both EX and CX are organised as a single function under one leader. They established this combined experience function at the time when Adobe began to focus more on customer service. This was because their business model was changing, from product sales to ongoing subscriptions and licensing. Although Adobe was well known for its products, they needed to drive a cultural shift, so they would also be known for providing excellent customer service.

In order to kick-start this transformation, they embedded customers' success measures into employees' performance management and rewards. They opened up customer feedback to all staff. For example, they set up "listening stations" which played back compelling customer stories.

They also ran hackathons (which they called "experience-a-thons") and invited non-technical staff. They found that feedback from non-technical staff was especially useful, as it was more like actual customers' feedback than the product-heavy comments coming from their own engineers.

The combined experience team at Adobe is also very closely tied to the marketing function, as they build a common brand and identity.

What both these examples show is that one important way of creating purpose and meaning is by building clear line of sight between employee experience and customer experience.

EX leaders inspire employees by making it clear how their job affects customers in positive ways.

2. EX is about learning and recognition

A second key dimension of EX leadership is a focus on learning. Feeling that you have an opportunity for personal growth is a strong predictor of employee engagement. It lies at the heart of employee experience. Providing chances for employee development is a core leadership and organisational capability.

Peter Senge made this point in his 1990 seminal book *The Fifth Discipline*. For Senge, a learning organisation is "a group of people working together collectively to enhance their capacities to create results they really care about." It's an essential capability for organisations to have in order to remain relevant and competitive.

I have always found *The Fifth Discipline* a very useful leadership guide. The key characteristics of a learning organisation have all been referred to at different points in this book, such as systems thinking, mastery, mental models and shared vision.

A learning organisation practices what Senge calls "team learning". There are three dimensions to team learning.

Firstly, it requires people to think deeply about complex issues. As such, it's about taking advantage of the collective wisdom of the team as a whole, rather than individual team members. Indeed, the focus of team learning overall is organisational development, not individual development.

Secondly, there is a need for innovative thinking and coordination. This requires high trust. Just like in great sports teams, "Outstanding teams in organisations develop operational trust where each team member remains conscious of other team members and can be counted on to act in ways that complement each other's actions."

Thirdly, learning teams focus on achieving their goals through building the capability and effectiveness of other groups in the organisation. By so doing, they improve overall performance as a result.

Team learning leads to personal growth, but it also makes organisations better equipped to solve problems and it ensures a better flow of information and ideas across organisational silos.

In team meetings, Senge argues, people learn best through conscious dialogue and discussion. Such an approach means people can tackle complex problems, develop innovative solutions and take coordinated action.

For Senge, dialogue and discussion are among the most critical of all leadership skills.

By creating true dialogue, "people become observers of their own thinking." Leaders need to help "team members to suspend their own assumptions." Helping to see each other as true colleagues "is critical to establish a positive tone and to offset the vulnerability that dialogue brings." To do all this well, it's important to recognise that team learning is a leadership skill that needs a lot of practice.

One of the key takeaways from Senge's work (others have made the same point) is that many organisations view learning and development very narrowly, for example, in terms of training and courses. Similarly, they view talent development very narrowly, in terms of building specific key competencies. And they view careers narrowly, in terms of traditional advancement and promotion. By contrast, the best companies view learning as a broad and fundamental organisational capability that is also a critical part of EX.

Individual experience maps

Senge's perspective opens up learning from an EX perspective, so that you can explore and take advantage of the wide array of moments that matter to individuals in terms of their own growth and development.

Many companies have adopted a simple formula to help with this, which is often called the 70-20-10 model. This says that roughly 70 per cent of professional growth comes from direct work experiences, 20 per cent comes from interactions with others, and only 10 per cent comes from formal training.

Too often, however, organisations and individuals latch on to the 10 per cent that is formal education. This becomes their main focus. Ensuring that you spend enough attention on the 70 per cent that is experiential and the 20 per cent that comes from interactions with others is important from both an organisational perspective and from the viewpoint of individual employees.

When it comes to organisations thinking about talent management, for example, Marc Effron is one of the leading proponents of experience-based approaches.

Leadership development can largely be thought of as giving the right people, the right experiences at the right time. But according to Marc, "Despite widespread recognition that experiences accelerate development, few companies use them as their development framework. Instead, managers and employees are left to struggle with complex and difficult-to-apply competency models."

A better approach is what Marc calls experience maps, which "accelerate job and career development by defining the specific experiences needed to excel in a role or function."

These learning maps are built through a deep understanding of the critical experiences that define success in particular key roles. Often that understanding comes from in-depth interviews with experts.

For example, many organisations struggle to develop general managers. They are often a talent group that is identified as mission-critical, but scarce.

This is because making the transition from functional leader to general manager is a difficult one. It involves switching from tactical to strategic execution. It requires developing a broad enterprise-wide perspective. Companies need a good pipeline of potential candidates and strong support structures to manage this well.

Finding good general managers is often a focus for talent management teams, who apply assessments and develop libraries of exacting competencies to measure candidates against.

Instead, it is possible to identify the core experiences that are required to be successful as a general manager. These might include things like designing and executing strategy, managing operations, financial management and people management.

Within each of these areas, there are specific experiences that should be attained, such as executing a restructuring plan or setting up an operation in a new country.

Through this kind of approach, you can also identify the "proving experiences" that are required for people to demonstrate the potential to move on to more challenging roles. These are moments of truth that reveal an individual's capability, for example, to lead a transformation programme.

Given just how fraught the science of measuring people's potential is, which is often done through surveys and assessments, this experience-based approach is also a reassuring addition.

The advantages of experience maps over traditional approaches are that they are easier for people (in other words, employees and job candidates) to understand, they are easier to assess, and they are more focused on results. In other words, they are clearer and more transparent.

Individual learning tools

There is also a benefit for individuals in thinking about their own learning experiences.

Over time, companies have placed more emphasis on individuals taking ownership of their self-development. As a result, it's become important for employees to build their own personal experience maps. Of course, they should be supported in doing this by their manager. But there is also now an array of journal-type technologies that are available to help and most modern Learning Management Systems now include experience mapping tools for employees.

The incorporation of these tools is part of an overall shift in performance and people management, away from annual or biannual reviews, to ongoing feedback, progress tracking, and goal adjustment.

From an EX point of view, these technologies provide a great source of data for tracking the effectiveness of your programmes. To what extent are learning experiences having a positive impact on team performance and employee engagement? Are there certain experiences or learning moments that are creating a positive lift among your key cohorts?

For example, by introducing a stronger review and reflection point at the end of a rotation in a graduate programme, are you getting a subsequent improvement in the overall effectiveness of that group? Are you also reducing the risk of people leaving after completing it? And through experimentation and iteration, can you identify the specific elements of that review process that have the greatest impact?

The people analytics team at Google, for example, identified the impact that a simple check list can have on discussions with new starters. They devised a series of prompts that were designed to make those initial discussions with managers more effective.

Google adopted a similar approach to performance management discussions, where people managers are given a structured approach (a one-page handout) in order to make those discussions more tangible and specific.

Later in this chapter, I make the point that EX leadership is about making small changes, which build momentum over time. This is exactly what Google found – that simple things, which were easy to produce, like check lists and manager guides, led to significant improvements in how staff viewed their development discussions.

Personalised learning

A check list is one way of providing structured advice. It can provide a framework within which managers can have an organised conversation regarding learning and development experiences.

Some organisations are also looking at how they can make this happen routinely and consistently through the use of personalised learning technologies. One key objective of these technologies is to operate relatively seamlessly, so they can make learning a part of your day-to-day job. It's possible, for example, to use bots in this way. These are sometimes envisioned as an interactive career coach.

A bot can collect and analyse information from employees and help answer learning and development questions. It's possible to use bots to direct employees to particular resources and to programmes that are a good fit for their goals. These recommendations can be based on an analysis of other people's progress, effectively matching opportunities to an individual's own skills and experiences.

Sometimes this software is referred to as a learning experience platform. For knowledge workers, in particular, who are sitting at a desk, it means people can access online resources and learn "in the flow of work." This is a phrase used by Josh Bersin and Marc Zao-Sanders (the CEO and co-founder of Filtered, an education-tech company). It recognises that, "For learning to really happen, it must fit around and align itself to working days and working lives. Rather than think of corporate learning as a destination, it's now becoming something that comes to us."

These platforms are part of a growing ecosystem of consumer-type tools for employees at work.

Bots can chat with internal applicants who are planning their next internal move and looking for assistance. They can be used to highlight internal job opportunities relevant to a candidate's current career experience, as the information can be integrated with your HR systems.

It's easy to see how this can be better than relying on someone manually checking an internal job board, seeing an alert, hearing about a job through the grapevine, or having it pointed out to them by their manager.

These "job dating" algorithms can be useful during a large-scale restructuring, when you need to identify the best opportunities for existing employees in a new organisation.

The advantage of bots is that they provide an instant reply, at any time of the day. They're also relatively affordable, and their effectiveness improves over time. They can be set up to run on internal social media and to integrate with HR systems.

They are a means of applying nudges in order to encourage people to take individual responsibility for their own learning. They can nudge an employee to consider learning options that they not have thought about before. After all, many people only have very limited time for reflecting on their own personal development options.

Technologies like these also potentially help tackle engrained bias and improve diversity in different roles, by providing greater openness around opportunities and resources.

However, there needs to be clear governance and human overview. There has to be a clear understanding of exactly how algorithms make recommendations. There needs to openness in terms of how and why these tools are being used and how you communicate about them. There has to be a clear review process in terms of efficacy, fairness and effectiveness.

The main advantage of these technologies is, in fact, that they can free up time.

Just as robotic automation is able to keep routine inquiries away from a call centre, so that employees can focus on harder-to-solve customer problems, so a career bot can deal with routine aspects of learning and development questions. This can then free up a managers' time, so they're able to dispense more thoughtful and personalised advice.

Reskilling for the future

Another focus for learning is on reskilling employees for the future of work. As described earlier in this book, many companies are planning for the kinds of jobs they will need in the future, especially as cognitive technologies come to prominence.

This often involves a process that begins with deconstructing your current jobs. This means looking at which job tasks are repetitive and independent, as these might better delivered through automation, and which tasks are more variable and interactive, as these are probably still best delivered by human beings.

Ravin Jesuthasan and John Boudreau in *Reinventing Jobs* argue that the best companies optimise the mix of specific tasks before automating them and that they also consider which human tasks need to be delivered by employees or through other worker types.

In terms of your future needs, a key talent pool is, of course, your current workforce. There are going to be general skill gaps in some of the areas that will be among the most important in the future. You can already see this in areas such as data science and data systems, for example. So many companies realise that their current employees are a great resource. They are proactive in helping them to reskill.

According to research by McKinsey, around 80 per cent of executives at medium and large size companies believe retraining and reskilling must be at least half of the answer to addressing their future skills gap.

Technology now exists that companies can use to understand their specific gaps and the degree to which they have the internal capacity to fill them.

It's possible to set out pathways for reskilling current employees who are in jobs that are at risk of automation. These are sometimes called job corridors or job transition pathways. Software can be used to analyse the mix of skills that people in your current roles already have and then compare that to the mix of skills that will be required in the future. These tools can then establish the steps that, for example, a bank teller can take in order to become an account executive in the future or that an accountant can take to be a data scientist, and so on.

At an aggregate level, these analyses can help organisations plan for their strategic workforce needs.

At an individual level, employees can be directed towards appropriate resources that are available on learning experience platforms.

The good news is that a recent study by the World Economic Forum found that "the average worker in the US economy has 48 viable job transitions."

The bad news is that the same report said: "But that figure falls to half that amount if they are looking to maintain or increase their current wages."

The human element in managing performance

In an EX world, there are many new and exciting opportunities for using technology and data to provide personalised learning. But in any organisation, the front-line manager remains the most critical element, and they will continue to be.

In fact, when using new technology, the focus should be on ways of freeing up time, so that people-focused conversations between employee and manager – at all levels of the organisation – are able to be more ongoing and consistent.

Effective and engaging managers take an interest in people's development. They have an interest in the people who work for them, full stop. But they are especially interested in thinking about how their team members can learn new things and achieve more as a result.

At a basic level, every manager can help employees understand how the business works. How does the company create value? What contributes to profit? What do customers want?

In so doing, they can involve employees by giving them access to fresh business information, such as sales, productivity, quality, customer feedback, and so on.

They can also build line of sight, so that an employee knows how they contribute to business goals and to the mission and purpose of the organisation.

These are all practical steps that contribute to the 70 per cent of effort that is related to experiential learning, and they are all manager-led.

The best companies really invest in people management. What does this mean?

It starts with selecting people who are good at it (or who have the potential to be good at it) into manager roles.

Too many people managers are "accidental managers" (to use the writer and trainer Gary Topchik's phrase). In other words, they have been promoted into people management positions on the basis of being good at their regular job (a good sales person or a good accountant, and so on).

To make matters worse, they're often given little management training on their first appointment. Leadership development programmes typically kick in far higher up the chain.

Investing in people management also means encouraging on-the-job coaching. Sometimes coaching is seen as the preserve of trained coaches, normally people with a background in psychology. But in simple terms, it means managers who are able to hold regular, meaningful conversations, and who can set clear, flexible and relevant goals.

A manager-coach tackles issues as they arise (rather than saving them up for formal appraisal meetings). They give lots of regular feedback and recognition.

If there is one people process that has an impact across the broadest range of EX moments, it is performance management. If you think about performance management broadly, then it's a chance to have a two-way conversation, to give structured feedback, to educate people about the business, to build line of sight, to set goals, to discuss career interests and development plans, and to recognise success.

Many organisations that have focused on EX have prioritised performance management first, because of this broad impact.

Performance management should be a process of frequent check-ins, setting and re-setting relevant goals, encouraging developmental conversations, and providing lots of real-time feedback and recognition.

There has been a growth in feedback tools to meet this demand. There are also a host of technologies which aim to gamify recognition, through online awards and certificates, and so on. Of course, an important aspect of recognition remains the informal and sincere "well done" from your manager.

For all these reasons, the human element is the most important part of any learning organisation. It's critical to focus on this, as well as technology, in order to combat the feeling that exists in many organisations, that learning and development is down to the employee.

In too many companies, "you're on your own" is still the prevailing philosophy. This is why only 63 per cent of employees in the UK say they "know what skills I need to develop to advance my career at my organisation." Far worse, only 35 per cent say their "organisation does a good job explaining how I can influence my career advancement."

Most companies have lots of opportunities to improve.

3. EX is personal

The third dimension in EX leadership is personalisation.

In terms of communications, this means designing and producing materials, preparing and delivering messages, in order to meet employees' individual requirements.

Three key elements stand out: providing personal content; when it matters to me; so that I can use the feedback to improve my experience.

The final aspect of making EX personal is the individual contribution that people make through their own behaviour and their own openness to feedback. This is the subject of the final chapter.

Content that's relevant for me

As consumers, we are used to personalised communications. Amazon recommends books to read. Netflix suggests movies to watch. Twitter highlights accounts to follow. On LinkedIn, I see posts that reflect my interests. On websites, I see adverts that are targeted at me.

These services are using algorithms that are utilising data collected through social media and via cookies that track my online activity. There's a payoff for me, in that it's now easier for me to find a good book to read, and so on. These services are using my data to provide personalised recommendations, which saves me time and effort.

Of course, it's not all upside. I might wonder how much my personal data is actually worth. I might be concerned about who else gets to use it. I could also worry that my choices, and the conversations that I have online, are getting narrower over time. There's a question over just how sophisticated these algorithms are and what kind of biases they contain. But most people seem to be fairly comfortable in agreeing to this kind of bargain generally.

Inside organisations, the bargain is still at a different stage of development. As described in the section on EX analytics above, many people are worried about their employer using their data in ways that feel intrusive. As a result, many companies are cautious about applying external social media methods, as they don't want to damage trust.

However, some organisations are beginning to use personalised communications to great effect. The first area you see this in is benefits and rewards, where employees are increasingly expected to think and act like consumers.

This consumerisation reflects the fact that more individual risk is being placed onto employees. At the very least, this means companies have a responsibility to help their staff make sensible and informed decisions. Given that consumption is the result of both rational decision-making and emotional factors, it's also incumbent upon employers to present choices in ways that reflect different styles of decision-making.

In the past, an employee may have received a total rewards statement on paper or by email. It probably read a bit like a bank statement. It detailed your benefits selections and summed up your total rewards. Employees probably had to log into a website at a fixed point in the year (normally the end of the calendar year or the tax year) to select their choices when it came to benefits.

In countries like the USA, where health care choices can vary widely, this is a critically important exercise for many people. In the UK and elsewhere, those choices are more likely to relate to things like pension contributions, insurance, vouchers and vacation days.

Most companies are now modernising their approach to rewards and benefits, reflecting the fact that employees' expectations – as consumers – are changing rapidly.

Increasingly, companies are providing choices that are more ongoing when it comes to benefits. This means employees can change their selections at times that are more convenient to them and that reflect key life events. Those events don't tend to run according to the tax year.

They're also doing more to inform and educate employees about topics such as personal finance and wellness, so that they're able to make better decisions. This is being delivered through an online experience that is more engaging and personalised. In other words, the software is intelligent enough to know a bit about your preferences and circumstances and can present options to you accordingly.

You can see how materials about pensions that will be useful to someone who is early in their career are going to be very different from someone who is closer to retirement age. The same goes for thinking about health and wellness. These are both very simple examples, but when you bundle together different analytics, you can develop sophisticated ways of personalising benefits information. It is possible to build in-depth personas that reflect a complex mix of demographic and other choice-based variables. These can be used to help shape and target material and to reflect different styles of communication.

Total rewards is the area – along with learning and development described earlier in this chapter – that many companies are focusing on first. This is because there are clear opportunities for efficiencies and cost savings and for the improving employees' experience. But over time, companies will move further in the direction of personalised communications in other areas, especially as the advantages are perceived by employees to outweigh the disadvantages.

Companies that are using internal social platforms like Workplace by Facebook, already have sophisticated tools for capturing employee preferences and interests. They provide a means for delivering personalised communications in creative and engaging ways.

This means that HR and Internal Communication functions need to work closely together. Both need to have an in-depth understanding of human behaviour and the ability to analyse data about their workforce.

They also need to adopt an approach to communications and behaviour change which is largely design-driven and iterative. Across a large workforce, for example, you might try different approaches for different groups, in order to analyse and learn more about what is working and why. Google calls this kind of approach "experimental marketing".

Those groups you identify may well be non-traditional, as in, they are based on in-depth personas that take account of multiple variables. Increasingly, technology can be used to re-design, re-deploy and re-test communications on a continuous basis.

For many companies this EX approach to personalising communications is still a long way off. Only 33 per cent of employees in the UK say "My organisation understands me as well as I am expected to understand our customers." Only 25 per cent say "The messages from my organisation seem like they are meant for me personally." This is an important area where many companies can up their game.

Moments that matter to me

One key aspect of personalisation, then, is targeting useful and relevant messages and materials at me. This means I don't have to search for information. I can be better informed. I can keep distractions to a minimum.

Personalisation is also about the timing of communications and the choices that I make. EX leadership is about making the most of the moments that matter to me.

A top-down view of the organisation implies that the timing of events, communication, and choices are dictated by management. Business updates reflect the financial calendar. Performance reviews are done close to year-end pay decisions. My opportunity to express my opinion is a two-week survey window that is set by management, typically in a quiet period for the business.

In a bottom-up EX world, things are flipped on their head.

Timing is determined by my schedule and my needs. I should be able to see how the business is doing, whenever I need to. I should get feedback when it's useful for me. I should be having discussions about how to improve my job performance in the moment of completing work. I should be able to give my opinion as and when things are happening. Information needs to flow continuously. I can listen and be listened to when it makes sense for me.

If you flip the organisation on its head like this, what are the milestones that might determine timings?

One key personal moment are anniversaries. This obviously includes the anniversary of when you joined the company. An EX approach to listening means you might be asked for your views on each anniversary. This might be a short survey delivered over social media. Perhaps you also receive some feedback when you do this, so you can reflect on your experience over the last year.

As a result of your feedback, you can be pointed towards resources. An anniversary is a natural moment to consider future learning opportunities. Of course, an anniversary is also a good time to be recognised for your achievements. This can come from your line manager, but also senior leaders as well.

Some companies are already adopting this kind of approach to employee listening. If you're a large company, it means that you're collecting feedback on engagement and commitment all the time, from across the organisation. This can be automated and bot-driven (in other words, chat-based).

Your joining date is only one kind of anniversary at work, of course. Other anniversaries that might matter to you include a promotion, completing a job rotation, a project that had been successfully accomplished, and so on.

Other key moments for connecting with employees include life events, such as returning after a period of maternity or paternity leave.

You can also focus on key business events like product launches and re-organisations.

The point is to shift your thinking, so that you're making the most of the memorable moments that matter to my experience at work.

Feedback that's useful for me

As well as connecting with me on a human level, and in the moments that really matter, a third key aspect of personalisation is giving feedback that's useful to me.

For example, when it comes to change management, a critical factor is communicating about What's In It For Me (WIIFM).

In sales and marketing, where the phrase originates, WIIFM means being clear on the value proposition for the audience and buyer. When it comes to leading change, it means ensuring that you cover the human side of making a transition, and thinking about the specific needs of teams and individuals.

This is something that William Bridges highlighted in his book *Managing Transitions*. His take on change leadership is insightful because he focuses on the human implications. In particular, he points out how changes in individuals' mindsets often lag far behind any organisational changes that are made. People go through different stages (letting go, a neutral zone, a new beginning) at their own pace, based on their experience.

It's hard to lead large-scale change successfully. Many companies struggle because they neglect to deal with the behavioural side.

Even in the first stage of a transition (letting go) there are multiple challenges you can face as people experience a range of emotions, including fear, denial, anger, uncertainty, and a sense of loss. This is why you typically see employee engagement scores drop in any organisation that is embarking on a major change.

Without support for dealing with this, front-line managers are put in a very difficult situation.

One typical coping strategy for team leaders is simply to hide and to communicate as little as possible. Another is to join employees in complaining about leadership and the bad decisions they make. This is the opposite of building an effective change coalition.

In order to head this off, there are key questions that you need to address from an employee experience perspective. These are personal and require a view of an individual's own experience in the company. They include things like: How will this impact me? How will it impact those around me? How will this benefit us? What can you tell me now? How can I contribute? What do I need to do differently?

Earlier in this book, we looked at the example of Philips, as it embarked on its Accelerate programme. As they completely restructured end-to-end processes in the company, they tackled these questions head on.

They embarked on a bottom-up listening strategy that equipped each team with a 100-day plan for how to do things differently in order to support the overall re-shaping of the business. They focused on employee experience and the process of managing personal transitions directly and to positive effect.

EX leadership means having engaging conversations where leaders listen with empathy and communicate as openly as they can about what's going on, even when it's challenging and difficult to do so.

10. EX has to be Authentic

Great EX leaders at all levels, then, make communications personal. They communicate in a way that is relevant and open, they make the most of the moments that matter, and they are clear about how changes affect me.

EX leadership is about instilling personalisation through the sensible use of technology and data. It is also about personalising the practice of leadership by leaders themselves.

This is the final capability in EX leadership and the end point for this book. In the end, EX leadership comes down to the personal contribution that people make through their own behaviour and their own openness to feedback.

Leadership that begins with me

I have deliberately kept this a broad statement. From an EX point of view, leadership refers to people at all levels, not just senior management.

To make leadership personal, you have to create a strong feedback culture. Individual feedback needs to be embedded in all your routines, across job levels.

As an employee, it's useful for me to get feedback from colleagues, my manager, customers, and elsewhere. Done right, and with support, this gives me a chance to reflect on what I can do differently and better.

For older workers, the way in which this is done is critical. As shown throughout this book, it has to be done in a way that builds trust. If you have long service with a company, there are potentially decades of mistrust to work through.

Younger generations tend to have more of an appetite for feedback. There is an expectation about getting it. For good and bad, on social media, feedback is everywhere.

There's an assumption, which is more and more common, that if you give feedback, then you should also get it. For example, I should get feedback when I give my views in a company employee survey. Tools exist now to enable this to happen. Based on my opinions, and what you have just learned about me, what resources are available to me that I can look at and how might I go about using them?

This thought process runs far deeper than just surveys: Through my use of internal social media and technology, what have you learned about how I like to receive information that you can pass back to me for my benefit? By looking at the courses I have taken and the projects I have completed, what do you recommend that I look at next?

I give feedback, I get feedback, I am supported to learn and adapt. This is a key way to build trust.

One of my favourite questions to ask in a team survey is simply: "What will you do differently to help our team achieve our goals?" Sceptical managers are always taken aback when they see the results, which are nearly always constructive. Even in the most troubled organisations, people are prepared to make a series of commitments. A manager can use these to co-create an effective action plan.

As a team leader, there should be accountability for receiving, giving and learning from feedback. Numerous examples in this book have shown how manager feedback needs to be embedded in your listening strategy. At Google, for example, manager feedback is shared and celebrated. It's a cornerstone of their culture.

For senior leaders, EX is a reflection of the kind of organisation they are looking to build. As such, the most important element in making EX personal, and therefore effective, is the ability of leaders to role model the required behaviours themselves. Sometimes this is referred to as authenticity.

There is a vast literature on authentic leadership that stretches back a long way. A lot of recent interest was inspired by Bill George's book *Authentic Leadership*. Written in 2003, the book was a response to growing criticism of corporate governance in the wake of scandals such as at Enron (the American energy trading company that collapsed after a massive accounting fraud scheme was revealed in 2001).

Dishearteningly, Enron had been celebrated as a successful organisation. The company had a clear code of ethics and a great-sounding set of values. However, in the end, these were clearly little more than words on a poster. Authentic leadership refers to making sure that values have deep roots.

Bill George (who was CEO of the medical technology company Medtronic) says authentic leaders are people who: "Lead with purpose, meaning and values. They build enduring relationships with people. Others follow them because they know where they stand. They are consistent and self-disciplined. When their principles are tested, they refuse to compromise. Authentic leaders are dedicated to developing themselves because they know that becoming a leader takes a lifetime of personal growth."

All these elements have been referred to at different points in this book. EX leadership requires purpose, learning and personalisation. It means leading by listening. It involves measuring the climate in different teams. It means understanding individual employee journeys. It requires team learning through discussion and dialogue. You need to make an effort to listen to all voices, including dissenting ones. This is why psychological safety is so important – making sure everyone can speak up. EX leadership requires consistency across all the moments that matter for building trust and confidence.

The most important component of EX leadership is leaders' own behaviours and consistency. Doing what you say, builds trust and confidence.

To improve cooperation, act collaboratively. To get great feedback, be good at giving it. When it comes to organisational change, break that change down into small pieces and show individuals the difference they can make by making those changes yourself.

This rule of small changes building over time is essential to EX as an emerging science. EX leadership is about taking lots of small steps in order to improve overall trust and performance. There is no one way ahead for all organisations. Companies will take different paths. But they always begin with small steps and learning from what's working and what's not.

That's why this book has taken the long-view of risk, trust, listening, engagement and experience. Where we are now is the result of lots of small steps that have already been taken by individual managers and employees. Where we will be in ten years' time will be the result of changes we make now.

We are only really at the beginning of building truly EX-focused organisations. We are learning which characteristics will stand us in good stead in the future.

Based on this long view of how we got here, one key mindset is thinking of conversation as leadership. You need to create an environment where it is safe to speak up. A conversation should be two-way. It's a chance for news and ideas to be exchanged. It requires carefully listening to other points of view. That may involve formal mechanisms like surveys and analytics, but listening can be done in lots of small ways too, many of them informal. Just being prepared to ask questions can start the ball rolling. For some leaders, this approach comes naturally, but for others it requires discipline, routines and practice.

Another key mindset is to embrace the human messiness of workplaces. You need to pay attention to both evidence and emotions. You need to make sure there is always a balance of logic and empathy when making decisions about people and organisations. The company's values and your own values should shape the way you make those decisions. Above all, remember that EX leadership is personal.

End Notes

The case studies in this book use information that is already publicly available. Sources include books, articles, websites, journals, newspapers, and so on. The key ones are mentioned below, organised by chapter.

In some cases, I have been able to also use information that has come directly from client sources, with their permission.

I would like to thank everyone I interviewed for this book, everyone who reviewed sections and gave me feedback, and everyone who helped me find useful information.

All errors are my own.

Chapter 2: Individual Risk and Trust

Pinker, Steven. *Enlightenment now: The case for reason, science, humanism, and progress*. Penguin Books, 2019.

Collins, James Charles, Jim Collins, and Jerry I. Porras. *Built to last: Successful habits of visionary companies*. Harper Business, 1994.

Worley, Christopher G., and Edward E. Lawler III. *Built to change: How to achieve sustained organisational effectiveness*. Jossey-Bass, 2006.

McAfee, Andrew, and Erik Brynjolfsson. *Machine, platform, crowd: Harnessing our digital future*. WW Norton & Company, 2017.

The figures for companies who fear they may become obsolete come from a study by Vanson Bourne & Dell Technologies. Results can be found online.

The figures on companies' plans for automation come from the Willis Towers Watson *Future of Work Survey* (2018) which you can find online.

On 47 per cent of jobs at threat, see Frey, Carl Benedikt, and Michael A. Osborne. "The future of employment: how susceptible are jobs to computerisation?" *Technological forecasting and social change* 114 (2017): 254-280.

The information on Coca-Cola, BMW and Alibaba comes from online sources.

Baldwin, Richard. *The globotics upheaval: Globalization, robotics, and the future of work.* Oxford University Press, 2019.

The workforce data in the UK comes from the Office for National Statistics (ONS).

The data on American retirement savings come from a survey reported in *Fortune* magazine in April 2018.

On trust, I have posted a full lit review in my Medium account @nick14.

In earlier drafts of this chapter, I also had a case study from another client, General Motors. But for reasons of space, I ended up taking it out. (You can still read it on my Medium account if you're interested.)

Hardin, Russell. *Trust.* Cambridge: Polity, 2006.

The General Social Survey (GSS) is a project of the independent research organisation NORC at the University of Chicago, with principal funding from the National Science Foundation.

The British Social Attitudes Survey is run by NatCen Social Research.

The Edleman Trust Barometer can be found on their website.

Pariser, Eli. *The filter bubble: What the internet is hiding from you.* Penguin, 2011.

Turkle, Sherry. *Reclaiming conversation: The power of talk in a digital age*. Penguin, 2016.

On trust in teams, see: Katzenbach, Jon R., and Douglas K. Smith. *The wisdom of teams: Creating the high-performance organisation*. Harvard Business Press, 1993. Tuckman, Bruce W. "Developmental sequence in small groups." *Psychological Bulletin* 63.6 (1965). Meyerson, Debra, Karl E. Weick, and Roderick M. Kramer. "Swift trust and temporary groups." *Trust in organisations: Frontiers of theory and research* 166 (1996).

On the performance impact of trust at a team level, see: De Jong, Bart A., Kurt T. Dirks, and Nicole Gillespie. "Trust and team performance: A meta-analysis of main effects, moderators, and covariates." *Journal of Applied Psychology* 101.8 (2016). Brown, Sarah, et al. "Employee trust and workplace performance." *Journal of Economic Behavior & Organization* 116 (2015): 361-378. Breuer, Christina, Joachim Hüffmeier, and Guido Hertel. "Does trust matter more in virtual teams? A meta-analysis of trust and team effectiveness considering virtuality and documentation as moderators." (2016).

Fukuyama, Francis. *Trust: The social virtues and the creation of prosperity*. Free Press Paperbacks, 1995.

On the impact on organisations, see: Zak, Paul J., and Stephen Knack. "Trust and growth." *The economic journal* 111.470 (2001): 295-321. Shleifer, A., La Porta, R., Lopez-de-Silanes, F., & Vishny, R. W. (1997). Trust in large organisations. *Am Econ Rev*, 87(2), 333-338. Goergen, Marc, et al. "Trust, owner rights, employee rights and firm performance." *Journal of Business Finance & Accounting* 40.5-6 (2013): 589-619.

On complexity, see: Morieux, Yves, and Peter Tollman. *Six simple rules: how to manage complexity without getting complicated*. Harvard Business Review Press, 2014. You can read about Gary Hamel's challenge to leaders on his website.

The Workplace Employment Relations Study (WERS) is a series of surveys that aims to provide a nationally representative account of the state of employment relations and working life inside British workplaces. You can find details on the WERS website. See also: Van Wanrooy, Brigid, et al. *Employment relations in the shadow of recession: Findings from the 2011 Workplace Employment Relations Study.* Macmillan, 2013.

The Skills and Employment Survey is a series of representative sample surveys of workers in Britain stretching back over 30 years. You can find details on the Cardiff University website. See also: Gallie, Duncan, et al. "Fear at work in Britain: first findings from the Skills and Employment Survey 2012." (2013).

The Americans' Changing Lives Study is the longest, ongoing national study in the US to clarify how community, work and social connections affect health throughout adulthood. You can find details on the University of Michigan website. See also: Burgard, Sarah A., and Sarah Seelye. "Histories of perceived job insecurity and psychological distress among older US adults." *Society and mental health* 7.1 (2017): 21-35.

Wartzman, Rick. *The end of loyalty: The rise and fall of good jobs in America.* Public Affairs, 2017.

On zero hours contracts, see: CIPD 2015 Policy Report, *Zero-hours and short-hours contracts in the UK: Employer and employee perspectives.*

The UCL study is summarised on their website under the heading "Being on a zero-hours contract is bad for your health." 5 July 2017.

Brendan Burchell's study is summarised on the University of Cambridge website under the heading "Zero-hours contracts are 'tip of the iceberg' of damaging shift work, say researchers". 18 Apr 2014. See also: Wood, A., and Brendan J. Burchell. "Zero hour contracts as a source of job insecurity amongst low paid hourly workers." (2014).

On workplace activism, see: "Workplace activism gathers pace after Ted Baker case" in *The Financial Times*, 17 January 2019.

The Willis Towers Watson data come from *The Global Workforce Survey* (2016).

You can find the CIPD Employee Outlook reports on their website.

Chapter 3: Safe to Speak Up

A lot has been written about Coca-Cola's transformation. For a short review of the development of the Manifesto for Growth at The Coca-Cola Company see the opening chapter in: Keller, Scott, and Colin Price. *Beyond performance: How great organisations build ultimate competitive advantage.* John Wiley & Sons, 2011. The long quote comes from an interview with Neville Isdell by Gregory Kesler: "How Coke's CEO aligned strategy and people to re-charge growth: an interview with Neville Isdell." *People & Strategy* 31.2 (2008): 18-22. For more on the impact of the Manifesto from a people perspective, also see: Fox, Adrienne. "Refreshing a beverage company's culture." *HR Magazine* 52.11 (2007): 58-60.

On Accelerate at Philips see: Mocker, Martin, and Eric van Heck. "Business-Driven IT Transformation at Royal Philips: Shedding Light on (Un) Rewarded Complexity." (2015). The transformation at Philips has been widely reported in the business press, such as: Tony Barber "Philips must learn to work as one unit" in *The FT*, July 4, 2013. See also Udo Kopka and Michiel Kruyt. "From Bottom to Top." *McKinsey Quarterly*, November 2014. Philips reported the key results from the My Accelerate Survey in its 2014 Annual Report, in the section on Engaging Our Employees.

You can read the Baker Panel report online. Baker, James, et al. "The report of the BP US refineries independent safety review panel." BP US Refineries Independent Safety Review Panel (2007). The report includes details of the safety culture survey. See also: MacKenzie, Cheryl, Donald Holmstrom, and Mark Kaszniak. "Human factors analysis of the BP Texas City refinery explosion." *Proceedings of the Human Factors and Ergonomics Society Annual Meeting.* Vol. 51. No. 20. Sage CA: Los Angeles, CA: Sage Publications, 2007. See also the 2008 CBS film "Anatomy of a Disaster" (a film produced by the U.S. Chemical Safety and Hazard Investigation Board, which features interviews with members of the investigative team).

On the dangers of practical drift, see Snook, Scott A. *Friendly fire: The accidental shootdown of US Black Hawks over northern Iraq.* Princeton University Press, 2002. On "the drift to danger" see also Rasmussen, Jens. "Risk management in a dynamic society: a modelling problem." *Safety science* 27.2 (1997): 183-213.

To be clear, I have not worked with NASA. All this information is public. The official report is by the Columbia Accident Investigation Board. "CAIB Report." *Washington, DC, August* (2003). See also Starbuck, William, and Moshe Farjoun, eds. *Organisation at the limit: Lessons from the Columbia disaster.* John Wiley & Sons, 2009.

On hubris, see: Owen, David, and Jonathan Davidson. "Hubris syndrome: An acquired personality disorder? A study of US Presidents and UK Prime Ministers over the last 100 years." *Brain* 132.5 (2009): 1396-1406. And: Claxton, Guy, David Owen, and Eugene Sadler-Smith. "Hubris in leadership: A peril of unbridled intuition?" *Leadership* 11.1 (2015): 57-78. Also see: de Vries, Manfred FR Kets, and Manfred FR Kets de Fries. *Prisoners of leadership.* Vol. 36. New York: Wiley, 1989.

This section also refers to: Rosenzweig, Phil. *The halo effect: and the eight other business delusions that deceive managers.* Simon and Schuster, 2014. On confirmation bias more generally, also see: Nickerson, Raymond S. "Confirmation bias: A ubiquitous phenomenon in many guises." *Review of general psychology* 2.2 (1998): 175. And: Plous, Scott. *The psychology of judgment and decision making.* Mcgraw-Hill Book Company, 1993.

Tedlow, Richard S. *Denial: Why business leaders fail to look facts in the face – and what to do about it.* Penguin, 2010.

Heffernan, Margaret. *Wilful blindness: Why we ignore the obvious.* Simon and Schuster, 2011.

On employee voice and silence, see the review by Elizabeth Wolfe Morrison from the Stern School of Business at New York University: Morrison, Elizabeth W. "Employee voice and silence." *Annu. Rev. Organ. Psychol. Organ. Behav.* 1.1 (2014): 173-197. See also: Dyne, Linn Van, Soon Ang, and Isabel C. Botero. "Conceptualising employee silence and employee voice as multidimensional constructs." *Journal of management studies* 40.6 (2003): 1359-1392. And: Morrison, Elizabeth Wolfe, and Frances J. Milliken. "Speaking up, remaining silent: The dynamics of voice and silence in organisations." *Journal of Management Studies* 40.6 (2003): 1353-1358.

Packard, David, David Kirby, and Karen R. Lewis. *The HP Way: How Bill Hewlett and I built our company.* New York: Harper Business, 1995.

Peters, Thomas J., Robert H. Waterman, and Ian Jones. *In search of excellence: Lessons from America's best-run companies.* Harper and Row, 1982.

On psychological safety, see Edmondson, Amy. "Psychological safety and learning behavior in work teams." *Administrative science quarterly* 44.2 (1999): 350-383. And also: Edmondson, Amy C. *Teaming to innovate.* John Wiley & Sons, 2013. You can also find a TED talk by Amy. You can read about the Google research online.

On fear-based silence see: Kish-Gephart, Jennifer & Detert, James & Klebe Treviño, Linda & Edmondson, Amy. "Silenced by fear: The nature, sources, and consequences of fear at work." *Research in organisational behaviour* 29 (2009): 163-193. See also: Detert, James R., and Amy C. Edmondson. *Everyday failures in organisational learning: Explaining the high threshold for speaking up at work.* Division of Research, Harvard Business School, 2005.

On Google see: Bock, Laszlo. *Work rules! Insights from inside Google that will transform how you live and lead.* Hachette UK, 2015. And: Schmidt, Eric, and Jonathan Rosenberg. *How Google works.* Hachette UK, 2014. For balance's sake and a different view, see: Vaidhyanathan, Siva. *The Googlization of everything (and why we should worry).* University of California Press, 2012.

Chapter 4. Employee Surveys

The poll about polls was reported on the Huff Post website on 31 March 2017. "A Poll Finds Most Americans Don't Trust Public Opinion Polls."

The size of the employee engagement industry in 2014 comes from Bersin at Deloitte.

On the emergence of the survey industry, see: Converse, Jean M. *Survey research in the United States 1890-1960.* Transaction

Publishers, 2011. And also: Groves, Robert M. "Three eras of survey research." *Public Opinion Quarterly* 85.5 (2011) 861-871.

Buckingham, Marcus, and Curt Coffman. *First, break all the rules: What the world's greatest managers do differently.* Simon and Schuster, 1999.

Herzberg, Frederick "One more time: how do you motivate employees." *Harvard Business Review* 46.1 (1968) 53-62.

Kahn, William A. "Psychological Conditions of Personal Engagement and Disengagement at Work." *The Academy of Management Journal* 33. 4 (1990): 692–724.

Meyer, John P., and Natalie J. Allen. "A three-component conceptualisation of organisational commitment." *Human resource management review* 1.1 (1991): 61-89.

Michaels, Ed, Helen Handfield-Jones, and Beth Axelrod. *The war for talent.* Harvard Business Press, 2001. (McKinsey launched its War for Talent research in 1997.)

Rucci, Anthony J., Steven P. Kirn, and Richard T. Quinn. "The employee-customer-profit chain at Sears." *Harvard Business Review* 76 (1998): 82-98.

Chapter 5. Employee Engagement

This chapter was not in my original book plan. But when I interviewed people for my book, they requested that I include case studies and pull out the key success factors in running engagement surveys. My interviewees pointed out that employee engagement surveys remain very common and that many companies struggle with them. So this is my list of the things that matter, based on what I have seen work well and not so well.

In this chapter I also refer to this book: Ulrich, Dave, David Kryscynski, Wayne Brockbank, and Mike Ulrich. *Victory through organisation: Why the war for talent is failing your company and what you can do about it.* McGraw Hill, 2017.

Chapter 6. Beyond Engagement

Schumpeter, J. *Capitalism, socialism and democracy*. Harper & Brothers, 1942.

The Conference Board publishes the results of its CEO Challenge surveys on its website. The results here are from the 2014 survey.

You can find the MacLeod report archived on the website of www.bis.gov.uk

Briner, Rob B. "What is employee engagement and does it matter? An evidence-based approach." The Future of Engagement Thought Piece Collection 51 (2014).

You can find Gallup's State of the Global Workplace reports on their website. These data come from the 2017 report. (Gallup Press).

Rosenzweig, Phil. *The halo effect: and the eight other business delusions that deceive managers*. Simon and Schuster, 2014

Young, Henry R., et al. "Who are the most engaged at work? A meta-analysis of personality and employee engagement." *Journal of Organisational Behavior* 39.10 (2018): 1330-1346. See also: "Is Employee Engagement Just a Reflection of Personality? by Tomas Chamorro-Premuzic. Lewis Garrad and Didier Elzinga in *Harvard Business Review*, 28 November 2018.

Barends, E., Rousseau, D.M., & Briner, R.B. (2014) *Evidence-Based Management: The Basic Principles*. Amsterdam: Centre for Evidence-Based Management.

You can see Rob Briner's 2014 article ("Don't believe the hype of employee engagement") on the website of HR Magazine.

The data on views of the effectiveness of employee surveys come from a HRmarketer report ("The Hypocrisy of Employee Surveys") which you can see on their website.

You can find the ONS data on their website.

Bruch, Heike, and Jochen I. Menges. "The Acceleration Trap." *Harvard Business Review* 88.4 (2010): 80-86.

You can find details on the Labour Force Survey on the HSE website.

On "hustle porn" see the article of the same name online at Thrive Global.

Page, Scott E. *The difference: How the power of diversity creates better groups, firms, schools, and societies.* Princeton University Press, 2008.

It's really worth visiting Vincent Granville's website Data Science Central for all sorts of data science questions. The quote here comes from his paper "Data Analysis to Data Science".

You can find Sean McClure's article ("Data Science and Big Data: Two very Different Beasts") on the KDnuggets website.

O'Neil, Cathy, and Rachel Schutt. *Doing data science: Straight talk from the frontline.* O'Reilly Media, 2013.

Marr, Bernard. *Big Data: Using SMART big data, analytics and metrics to make better decisions and improve performance.* John Wiley & Sons, 2015.

The IKEA research comes from a conference presentation.

Chapter 7. Employee Experience

Morgan, Jacob. *The employee experience advantage*: John Wiley & Sons, 2017.

Maylett, Tracy, and Matthew Wride. *The employee experience: How to attract talent, retain top performers, and drive results.* John Wiley & Sons, 2017.

Pennington, Alan. *The customer experience book: How to design, measure and improve customer experience in your business.* Pearson, 2016.

Pine, B. Joseph, Joseph Pine, and James H. Gilmore. *The experience economy: work is theatre & every business a stage.* Harvard Business Press, 1999. See also: Pine, B. Joseph, and James H. Gilmore. "Welcome to the experience economy." *Harvard Business Review* 76 (1998): 97-105.

Solis, Brian. *X: The experience when business meets design.* John Wiley & Sons, 2015.

You can view the Deloitte 2016 *Global Human Capital Trends Report* on their website.

Effron, Marc. *Still Under Construction: The State of HR Analytics 2016.* New Talent Management Network, 2016.

Marler, Janet H., and John W. Boudreau. "An evidence-based review of HR Analytics." *The International Journal of Human Resource Management* 28.1 (2017): 3-26.

Levenson, Alec, and Gillian Pillans. *Strategic Workforce Analytics.* The Corporate Research Forum, November 2017.

The data on gender pay gap errors was reported in *The Times* on 23 April 2019, "Hundreds of errors mar pay gap data".

Josh Bersin in *Forbes* on 26 August 2015: "Feedback is the Killer App: A New Market and Management Model Emerges." Available on their website.

Revella, Adele. *Buyer personas: how to gain insight into your customer's expectations, align your marketing strategies, and win more business.* John Wiley & Sons, 2015.

Simon, Herbert A. *The sciences of the artificial.* Cambridge, 1969.

Brown, T. *Change by design: How design thinking transforms organisations and inspires innovation.* Harper Business, 2009.

Chapter 8: EX: An Emerging Science

Kleven, Henrik, Camille Landais, and Jakob Egholt Søgaard. *Children and gender inequality: Evidence from Denmark.* No. 24219. National Bureau of Economic Research, 2018.

Senge, Peter M. *The fifth discipline: The art and practice of the learning organisation.* Random House, 1990.

Sterman, John D. *Business dynamics: systems thinking and modeling for a complex world.* McGraw-Hill. 2000.

Parsons, Talcott. *The social system.* Macmillan, 1964.

For a great take on a systems thinking view of employee engagement, see the paper "A dynamic approach to employee engagement" by Andrew Marritt which was published on his

LinkedIn page on 10 December 2015. You can also read his paper "Fixing employee engagement (and why we've been doing it wrong)" online (including on the Unleash IO website).

You can find more information on these companies' pulse surveys online. For example: Eugene Kim, "Amazon employees start their day by answering a simple question about work." (This is on the CNBC website: 20 March 2018). The quotes included in this section, come from here. See also: Scott Judd, Eric O'Rourke, and Adam Grant. "Employee Surveys Are Still One of the Best Ways to Measure Engagement." *Harvard Business Review*, March 14, 2018. The information on the Twitter survey comes from a 2016 conference presentation.

For a good view on the importance of focusing on social relations in the modern workplace, see Jon Ingham's book *The social organisation*. Kogan Page, 2017.

Jennings, Helen Hall. *Leadership and isolation: A study of personality in interpersonal relations*. Longman, 1943.

For a good review of recent work in SNA, see David Green's article "The role of Organisational Network Analysis in People Analytics" which you can find on LinkedIn or on his blog.

Josh Bersin in *Forbes* August 26, 2015: "Feedback is the Killer App: A New Market and Management Model Emerges." Available on their website.

Nudge theory is associated with the work of Richard Thaler, for example: Thaler, Richard H., and Cass R. Sunstein. *Nudge: Improving decisions about health, wealth, and happiness*. Penguin, 2009.

McChrystal, General Stanley, Tantum Collins, David Silverman, and Chris Fussell. *Team of teams: New rules of engagement for a complex world*. Penguin, 2015.

The MBA study comes from: Emily Drefuss. "For Women Job Seekers, Networking Like a Man Isn't Enough." Featured in *Wired*, 21 January 2019.

This is a good report on open plan offices: "When the walls come down: How smart companies are rewriting the rules of the open workplace" by Oxford Economics (available on their website).

The figures on London office space come from a study by Seaforth Land, a London property investor, which was reported in *The Financial Times* on March 31, 2019. Seaforth's figures are based on underlying data from CBRE, a property agency, and EGi, a data service. Various forces are reflected in these trends, including hot desking, more use of freelancers, a reduction in the amount of physical filing space required, improved space utilisation technology, the emergence of short-term work desks for hire through firms like We Work, etc.

On Glassdoor, see: Rolfe Winkler and Andrea Fuller. "How Companies Secretly Boost Their Glassdoor Ratings." *Wall Street Journal*, 22 January 2019.

On the correlation of Glassdoor ratings and employee engagement, see the great paper by Jason McPherson, "Predicting Glassdoor scores with engagement data" which can be found on the cultureamp website (blog pages).

The data on advocacy come from LinkedIn and their report "The Network Effect of Employee Advocacy" which can be found online.

On NPS, see: Reichheld, Frederick F. "The one number you need to grow." *Harvard business review* 81.12 (2003): 46-55. And also: Reichheld, Fred. *The ultimate question*. Harvard Business School Press, Boston, MA (2006).

For a good critical review of employee NPS see: "Net Promoter Score (NPS) won't work for HR, Net Activated Value (NAV) will" by Mike West, which you can find on his LinkedIn page, published on 14 July 2016.

Maylett, Tracy, and Matthew Wride. *The employee experience: How to attract talent, retain top performers, and drive results*. John Wiley & Sons, 2017.

Morgan, Jacob. *The employee experience advantage*: John Wiley & Sons, 2017.

Pennington, Alan. *The customer experience book: How to design, measure and improve customer experience in your business*. Pearson, 2016.

On high the contribution of high performers, see Francesca Gino "The Problem with Being a Top Performer" in *Scientific American*

July 5, 2017. See also: Lazear, Edward P., Kathryn L. Shaw, and Christopher T. Stanton. "The value of bosses." *Journal of Labor Economics*. 33.4 (2015): 823-861.

The Deloitte figure comes from: Josh Bersin, "Employee Retention Now a Big Issue: Why the Tide has Turned", LinkedIn Article, 2013.

On IBM's predictive attrition algorithm, see the article on CNBC's website, "IBM artificial intelligence can predict with 95 per cent accuracy which workers are about to quit their jobs" published on 3 April 2019. See also the article by Josh Bersin, "What emails reveal about your performance at work" which is available on his website, published 16 October 2018.

See the Accenture paper "Putting Trust to Work" which is on their website.

See the article: "Telegraph removes desk sensor monitors overnight following staff uproar" on the Press Gazette website.

On the bias in AI, see the excellent book by Cathy O'Neill. *Weapons of math destruction: How big data increases inequality and threatens democracy*. Broadway Books, 2017.

On cyber defence AI, see the article: "System predicts 85 per cent of cyber-attacks using input from human experts" on the MIT News website (April 18, 2016).

See: The Schumpeter article in *The Economist* of 10 September, 2015: "Digital Taylorism: A modern version of "scientific management" threatens to dehumanise the workplace".

Chapter 9. EX Leadership

For a view on the history of The Coca-Cola Company in this period, read: Constance Hays, *The real thing: Truth and power at The Coca-Cola Company*. Random House, 2005. And for a longer view, see also: Mark Pendergrast, *For God, Country, and Coca-Cola*. Basic Books, 2013. These quotes from Neville Isdell come from an interview with *The Belfast Telegraph* by Fearghal O'Connor, 15 August 2017. The *Fortune* article mentioned is this one: "The Real Story: How did Coca-Cola's management go from first-rate to farcical in six short years?" By Betsy Morris, May 31, 2004.

Jayne-Anne Gadhia's autobiography is: *The Virgin Banker*. Virgin Books, 2018.

These quotes from Fisk Johnson come from the company's website.

Collins, James Charles, Jim Collins, and Jerry I. Porras. *Built to last: Successful habits of visionary companies*. Harper Business, 1994.

Kay, John. *Obliquity: Why our goals are best achieved indirectly*. Profile Books, 2011.

Schwartz, Barry. *Why we work*. Simon & Schuster, 2015.

Pfeffer Jeffrey. *The human equation: Building profits by putting people first*. Harvard Business Press, 1998.

Ariely, Dan. *Payoff: The hidden logic that shapes our motivations*. Simon & Schuster, 2016.

Pink, Daniel H. *Drive: The surprising truth about what motivates us*. Penguin, 2011.

Duckworth, Angela. *Grit: The power of passion and perseverance*. Scribner, 2016.

Survey data in this chapter come from the Willis Towers Watson *Global Workforce Study*.

Berg, Justin M., Jane E. Dutton, and Amy Wrzesniewski. "Job crafting and meaningful work." *Purpose and meaning in the workplace* 81 (2013): 104.

See also: Wrzesniewski, Amy, et al. "Job crafting and cultivating positive meaning and identity in work." *Advances in positive organisational psychology*. Emerald Group Publishing, 2013.

Bakker, A. B., & Demerouti, E. (2018). "Multiple levels in job demands-resources theory: Implications for employee well-being and performance." In E. Diener, S. Oishi, & L. Tay (Eds.), *Handbook of wellbeing*. DEF Publishers.

On the Toyota Production System, see: Ohno, Taiichi. *Toyota production system: beyond large-scale production*. Productivity Press, 1988.

On Airbnb see: Denise Lee Yohn, "Fuse Customer Experience and Employee Experience to Drive Your Growth" on *Forbes* online, 6 March 2018.

On Adobe see: Jeanne Meister, "The Future of Work: Airbnb CHRO Becomes Chief Employee Experience Officer" on *Forbes* online, 21 July 2015.

Senge, Peter M. *The fifth discipline: The art and practice of the learning organization*. Random House, 1990.

See: Marc Effron, "A Simple Way to Map Out Your Career Ambitions." *Harvard Business Review*, 30 November 2018.

"Learning in the flow of work" is a phrase used by Josh Bersin and Marc Zao-Sanders in their article "Making Learning a Part of Everyday Work". *Harvard Business Review*, 19 February 2019.

Ravin Jesuthasan and John Boudreau. *Reinventing jobs: A 4-step approach for applying automation to work*. Harvard Business Press, 2018.

The January 2018 article: "Retraining and reskilling workers in the age of automation" by Pablo Illanes, Susan Lund, Mona Mourshed, Scott Rutherford, and Magnus Tyreman is available on the McKinsey website.

World Economic Forum Insight Report: *Towards a Reskilling Revolution: A Future of Jobs for All*. January, 2018

For a good book on engaging managers, see: Gebauer, Julie, Don Lowman, and Joanne Gordon. *Closing the engagement gap: How great companies unlock employee potential for superior results*. Penguin, 2008. They also use this idea of an "informed, sincere thank you" as a key ingredient in recognition and engagement.

Topchik, Gary S. *The accidental manager: get the skills you need to excel in your new career*. Amacom Books, 2004.

Bridges, William. *Managing transitions: Making the most of change*. Da Capo Press, 1991.

10. EX has to be Authentic

In terms of the appetite for more frequent feedback, see the report by Oxford Economics and SAP "A Millennial Misunderstanding" which you can find on the Oxford Economics website.

George, William W. *Authentic leadership: Rediscovering the secrets to creating lasting value.* Jossey-Bass, 2003.

See also: Gardner, William L., et al. "Authentic leadership: A review of the literature and research agenda." *The leadership quarterly* 22.6 (2011): 1120-1145.

Please note that for more information, including more papers and sources, you can also view my pages on Medium @nickl4 and on Research Gate.

About the Author

Nick Lynn has spent twenty years as a consultant helping companies improve engagement and employee experience. He has a PhD from the University of Birmingham and was as a Lecturer at the University of Edinburgh, where he is an Honorary Fellow. He joined the employee survey firm ISR (International Survey Research) in 1999, working in London, Chicago and New York. He regularly blogs and presents at conferences. You can follow him on Medium and Twitter @nickl4 and on LinkedIn at linkedin.com/in/nicklynn and also via his website: www.exleadership.com

Printed in Great Britain
by Amazon

27682347R00138